750.92 £6.95

JUDITH CLARKE    74 MARGARET RD  ST JOHNS WORCS
421174.

Evesham + Malvern Hills College.

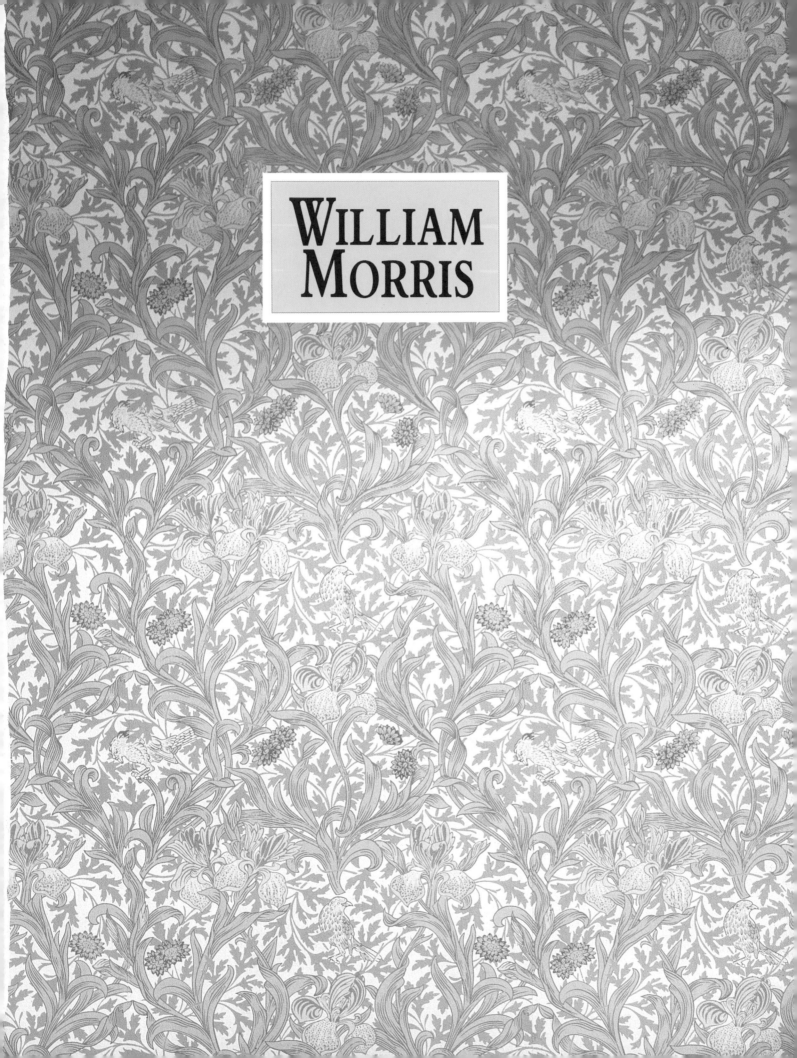

# WILLIAM MORRIS

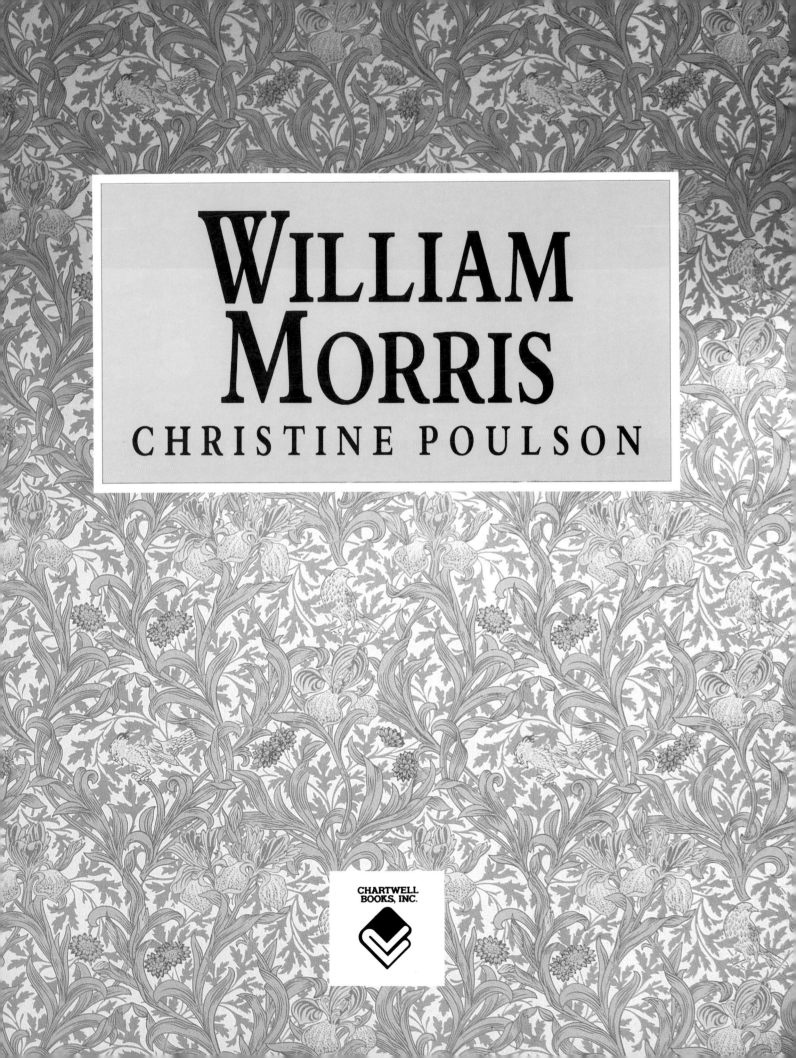

# WILLIAM MORRIS

## CHRISTINE POULSON

CHARTWELL
BOOKS, INC.

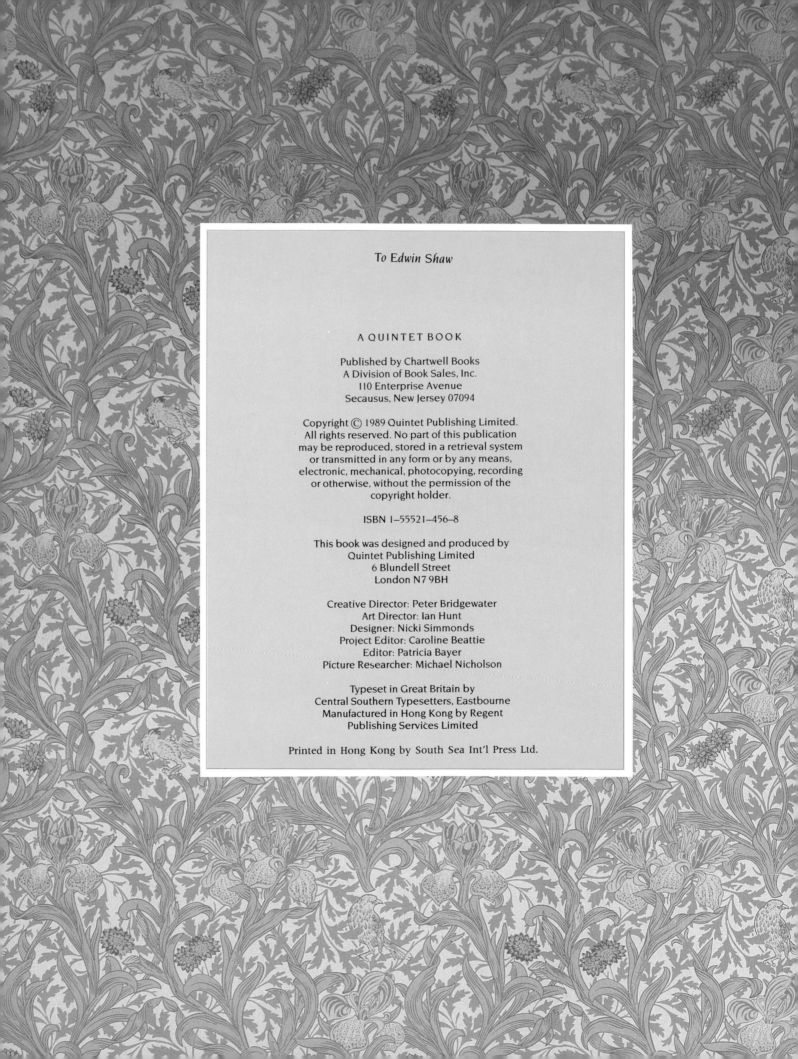

*To Edwin Shaw*

A QUINTET BOOK

Published by Chartwell Books
A Division of Book Sales, Inc.
110 Enterprise Avenue
Secausus, New Jersey 07094

ISBN 1–55521–456–8

This book was designed and produced by
Quintet Publishing Limited
6 Blundell Street
London N7 9BH

Creative Director: Peter Bridgewater
Art Director: Ian Hunt
Designer: Nicki Simmonds
Project Editor: Caroline Beattie
Editor: Patricia Bayer
Picture Researcher: Michael Nicholson

Typeset in Great Britain by
Central Southern Typesetters, Eastbourne
Manufactured in Hong Kong by Regent
Publishing Services Limited

Printed in Hong Kong by South Sea Int'l Press Ltd.

# CONTENTS

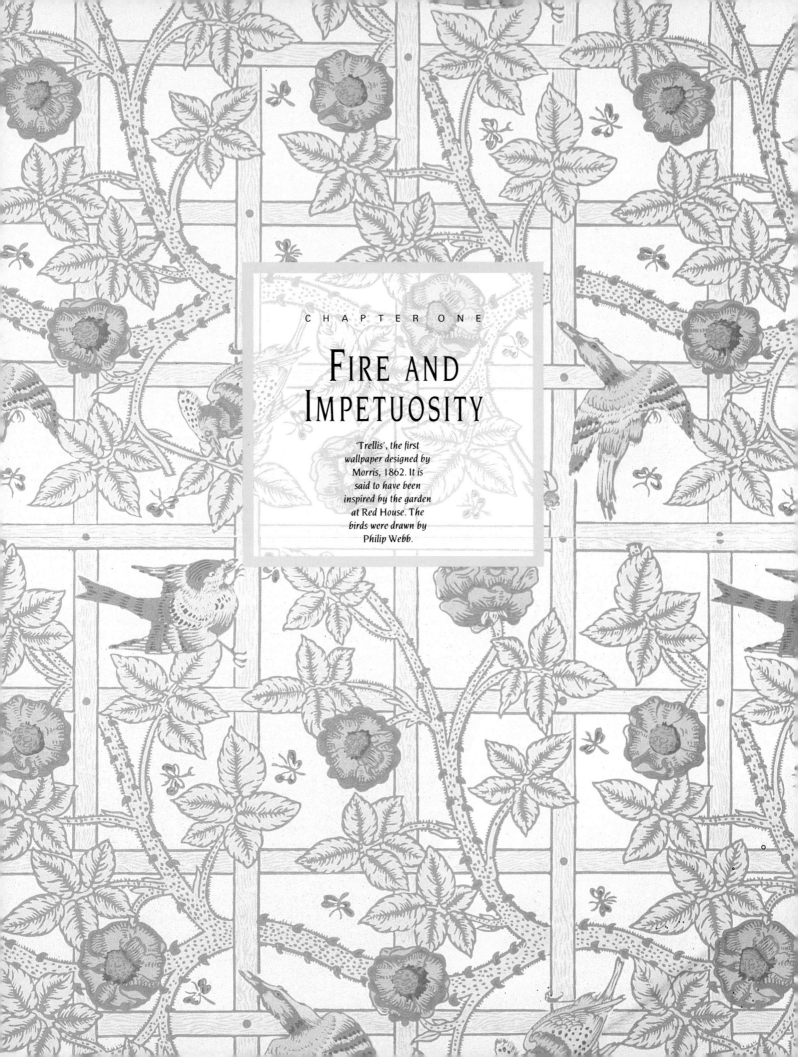

# CHAPTER ONE

# FIRE AND IMPETUOSITY

'Trellis', the first
wallpaper designed by
Morris, 1862. It is
said to have been
inspired by the garden
at Red House. The
birds were drawn by
Philip Webb.

RIGHT *Water House, Walthamstow, now the William Morris Gallery, the home of the Morris family from 1848 to 1856.*

WHEN WILLIAM MORRIS DIED at the age of 62 on 3 October 1896, an eminent doctor wrote: 'I consider the case is this: the disease is simply being William Morris, and having done more work than most ten men'. Morris was indeed a man of prodigious energy and versatility; any single one of his activities would have totally exhausted the energies of a lesser man. Part of his genius lay in his intense vitality. In his own day he was famous as a poet and as a designer of wallpapers, textiles and furniture, and notorious as a fiercely committed socialist. He founded the Society for the Protection of Ancient Buildings, which is still active today, and was one of the first to translate the Icelandic sagas into English. Although a sick man, in the last few years of his life he still had the energy to explore a whole new area of design, that of printing and typography, and to establish the Kelmscott Press.

William Morris came from a privileged, solidly middle-class background. He was born on 24 March 1834, the third of nine children, at Elm House, Walthamstow. Elm House was an unpretentious Georgian building with a fine garden; Walthamstow, now on the northeastern fringe of London, was then a pleasant country village. Morris's father was a partner in a successful firm of discount brokers. The firm prospered, and in 1840, when Morris was six, the family moved to a grander house.

Woodford Hall was a large and impressive Georgian residence on the edge of Epping Forest. Later in life Morris claimed to have known Epping Forest yard by yard as a boy. He was a precocious child; according to JW Mackail, his first biographer, he was reading the novels of Sir Walter Scott by the age of four. Morris's childhood was a happy and uneventful one, spent reading, riding his pony in the forest in a toy suit of armour, fishing with his brothers. He loved the wildness of Epping Forest and also the old Essex churches and countryside, whose architecture he was able

WOODFORD HALL. ESSEX.

RIGHT *Elm House, Walthamstow, Morris's birthplace, from a drawing by E H New (1871– 1931).*

to appreciate even as a child. At the age of eight he visited Canterbury Cathedral with his father and later recalled 'thinking that the gates of heaven had been opened to me'. Another early memory was of the tapestry hanging in Queen Elizabeth's Lodge in Epping Forest; he long remembered 'a room hung with faded greenery' and 'the impression of romance that it made upon me!'

Morris's father died in 1847; thanks to a lucky investment in copper mining a few months previously, his family was left very well provided for. Nevertheless, they soon moved to more modest accommodation at the Water House, Walthamstow, now the William Morris Gallery. Here they stayed until 1856. Shortly after his father's death Morris left his preparatory school in Walthamstow to go to Marlborough College, one of the new public schools which proliferated in the mid-19th century. Hastily set up to meet the demands of the expanding middle classes, some of these

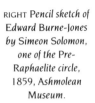

RIGHT *Pencil sketch of Edward Burne-Jones by Simeon Solomon, one of the Pre-Raphaelite circle, 1859, Ashmolean Museum.*

establishments were ramshackle, even disreputable. Morris himself, in a brief autobiographical passage which he wrote in a letter of 1883, described Marlborough as a:

> *. . . very rough school. As far as my school instruction went, I think I may fairly say I learned next to nothing there, for indeed next to nothing was taught; but the place is in very beautiful country, thickly scattered over with prehistoric monuments, and I set myself eagerly to studying these and everything else that had any history in it, and so perhaps learnt a good deal.*

The only serious influence which Marlborough had on Morris was to turn him from the Evangelicalism of his family towards Anglo-Catholicism. This influence was reinforced by the Rev FB Guy, an Anglo-Catholic clergyman who was Morris's tutor for almost a year after he left Marlborough in 1851. At this time a strong Anglo-Catholic party existed within the Church of England, brought into being in the 1830s by the Oxford Movement. Begun as a call for moral seriousness within the Church of England by three young Oxford clerics – John Henry Newman, John Keble and Edward Pusey

– the Oxford Movement demanded a restoration of ceremony and emphasized the importance of service among the poor. This combination of idealism and a nostalgic longing to give back to the church the importance which it was seen as having in medieval times was a potent one for Morris. He went up to Exeter College, Oxford, in 1853, determined to prepare for a career as an Anglo-Catholic clergyman.

Within a few days of arriving in Oxford, Morris met Edward Burne-Jones (1833–98) and immediately formed with him a friendship which was to last for life. Burne-Jones later drew a vivid picture of the young Morris as he knew him at Oxford: 'From the first I knew how different he was from all the men I had ever met. He talked with vehemence, and sometimes with violence. I never knew him languid or tired. He was slight in figure in those days; his hair was dark brown and very thick, his nose straight, his eyes hazel-coloured, his mouth exceedingly delicate and beautiful.' Burne-Jones introduced him to his own circle of friends who had been at school with him in Birmingham – Richard Dixon, Charles Faulkner (who was to become a lifelong friend and colleague) and William Fulford.

All five men had been profoundly influenced by the Oxford Movement and intended to take holy orders, although only Fulford and Dixon did so, the latter becoming a canon. This group formed a set which met in Faulkner's rooms in Pembroke College to discuss literature and theology. 'In no long time . . .', recalled Canon Dixon, 'the great characters of his [Morris's] nature began to impress us. His fire and impetuosity, great bodily strength, and high temper were soon manifested: and were sometimes astonishing. As, e.g., his habit of beating his own head, dealing himself vigorous blows, to take it out of himself'. Morris always had great physical energy, which at Oxford found an outlet in boating and fencing.

LEFT *Morris at Oxford, aged* 23.

RIGHT *John Everett Millais*, The Return of the Dove to the Ark, *1851, oil on canvas, Ashmolean Museum. When Morris and Burne-Jones saw this picture in 1854 its freshness and originality was a revelation to them.*

LEFT *Rossetti's watercolour*, Dante Drawing an Angel on the Anniversary of the Death of Beatrice, *1853–4, Ashmolean Museum. This was the picture which most impressed Morris and Burne-Jones when they visited the collection of Mr Combe, head of the Clarendon Press in Oxford.*

Both Morris and Burne-Jones had expected to find Oxford alive with religious fervour and were disappointed by the apathy and indifference which they encountered there. Together they read widely: Chaucer, Tennyson, Keats, Newman, Carlyle, Ruskin. They examined the medieval illuminated manuscripts in the Bodleian Library. They both agreed with Carlyle that the Middle Ages, in particular its religious communities, offered a model for organizing society which was better than the industrialization and urbanization of the present. So much in earnest were they that when Morris came of age in 1854 and inherited £900 a year, he planned at first to use his fortune to found a monastery or a quasi-monastic brotherhood along the lines of a community established by Newman at Littlemore, near Oxford, in the 1840s.

In the summer of 1855 both Morris and Burne-Jones abandoned their plans to enter the church. They had become increasingly interested in art. Ruskin's *Edinburgh Lectures*, published in 1854, first introduced them to the Pre-Raphaelites. Burne-Jones recalled: 'I was working in my room when Morris ran in one morning bringing the newly published book with him: so everything was put aside until he read it all through to me. And there we first saw about the Pre-Raphaelites ... So for many a day after that we talked of little else but paintings which we had never seen ...'. This state of affairs did not last long: the first Pre-Raphaelite painting which Morris and Burne-Jones saw was Millais' *The Return of the Dove to the Ark* of 1851, which was exhibited in a shop in Oxford in 1854. The freshness and originality of this picture were a revelation to them: 'and then ... we knew', in Burne-Jones's words. They got permission to see the Pre-Raphaelite pictures in the collection of Mr Combe, head of the Clarendon Press at Oxford; here their

RIGHT *Church of St. James-the-Less, Lillington Gardens, Vauxhall Bridge Road, designed by the Gothic Revivalist architect G E Street, 1859–61. Morris was apprenticed to Street in 1856 and spent about nine months working in his office.*

LEFT *Drawing of Rouen Cathedral by John Ruskin, c. 1850. Morris greatly admired the Gothic cathedrals of Northern France and said of Rouen cathedral, 'no words can tell you how its mingled beauty, history and romance book hold of me . . . It was the greatest pleasure I ever had'. Ruskin, whose writings on art and architecture influenced Morris so much, was a fine amateur artist.*

'greatest wonder and delight are reserved for a water-colour of Rossetti's, of Dante drawing the head of Beatrice and disturbed by people of importance'.

What they now saw was that the moral seriousness, the inspiration and the direction in life which they so earnestly sought might be found not in religion, as they had first supposed, but in art. The two men did not relinquish their religious vocations without a struggle, but during a trip to northern France in 1855 the decision was finally taken. Morris had already visited France the previous summer and had been much moved by the power of the great Gothic cathedrals of Chartres, Beauvais, Amiens and Rouen. In his 1887 lecture, 'The Aims of Art', he referred to the time when 'I first saw the city of Rouen, then still in its outward aspect a piece of the Middle Ages: no words can tell you how its

mingled beauty, history and romance took hold on me; I can only say that, looking back on my past life, I find it was the greatest pleasure I ever had . . .'. Now he returned with Burne-Jones for a holiday which marked a turning point in both their lives . Burne-Jones recalled:

> . . . it was while walking on the quay at Havre at night that we resolved definitely that we would begin a life of art, and put off our decision no longer – he [Morris] would be an architect and I a painter. It was a resolve only needing a final conclusion; we were bent on that road for the whole past year, and after that night's talk we never hesitated more. That as the most memorable night of my life.

Morris left university as soon as possible with a pass degree, apprenticing himself to the Gothic Revival architect, GE Street, who had his office in Oxford. He began work there in January 1856 and stayed only about nine

LEFT *Portrait of Dante Gabriel Rossetti by William Holman Hunt, oil on wood, 1853. In 1856 Morris met Rossetti and, guided by him, decided to take up painting rather than architecture.*

RIGHT T*he* If I Can *woollen hanging, designed and embroidered by Morris at Red Lion Square, now at Kelmscott Manor. 'If I can' was the motto of the fifteenth century Flemish painter Van Eyck, whom Morris much admired. Morris adopted it as his own.*

months. The work which he was given – copying a detailed drawing of the doorway of St Augustine's, Canterbury – he found tedious. Nevertheless, the experience was a useful one and reinforced Morris's view of architecture as the most important of the visual arts. A lifelong friendship was begun in Street's office with Philip Webb (1831–1915), the chief assistant, who was later to be the architect of Morris's first married home and Morris's co-worker in the Society for the Protection of Ancient Buildings. Webb vividly recalled meeting the young Morris, 'a slim boy like a wonderful bird just out of his shell'.

Even by Morris's standards, this was a year of intense activity. In January the first number of T*he* Oxford *and* Cambridge Magazine appeared,

financed by Morris, who paid a salary of £100 a year to Fulford to act as editor. This was a journal produced by Morris, his circle at Oxford and other friends at Cambridge; it was modelled on T*he* Germ, the Pre-Raphaelite journal which had appeared in 1850. Of the 12 monthly numbers which appeared in 1856, only two did not contain a contribution by Morris. His offerings were quite varied, including eight prose romances, an article on Amiens cathedral and some of the poetry which he had begun to write prolifically as an undergraduate; nevertheless, Morris's deep love of the medieval found expression in almost all of them. This was a source of inspiration which was to last for the rest of his life. It was not simple escapism; as Burne-Jones remarked,

LEFT Topsy and
Ned Jones Settled
on the Settle in
Red Lion Square,
*wash drawing, 1916,
by Max Beerbohm.
Morris designed the
settle which was
decorated with designs
by Rossetti. It is now
in Red House.*

'all his life, he hated the copying of ancient work as unfair to the old and stupid for the present, only good for inspiration and hope.' Some of Morris's greatness, particularly as a designer, lay in his ability to use inspiration from the work of the past to create something entirely new. This is true, too, of the best of his early poetry, in which medieval themes are treated with startling vigour and vividness to produce work which is entirely original.

In the summer of 1856 Street moved his office to London, so Morris was able to leave Oxford and move into lodgings in Upper Gordon Street, Bloomsbury, with Burne-Jones (who had already moved to London). In January 1856 Burne-Jones had managed to engineer a meeting with Dante Gabriel Rossetti (1828–82),

who was the most important figure of the Pre-Raphaelite Brotherhood to Morris and to himself, and by May he had moved to London to become his pupil on an unofficial basis. Rossetti had by this time moved away from the style which they had so much admired in Millais' *The Return of the Dove to the Ark*. The early stage of Pre-Raphaelitism which had been concerned with an earnest and iconoclastic insistence on painting from nature, on minute attention to detail over the whole canvas and on fresh, vivid colours had demanded a technical competence for which Rossetti was ill-equipped. He had been discouraged by the poor critical response to his early pictures. He was now engaged on a series of small esoteric watercolours on medieval and chivalric themes.

RIGHT *Arthur
Hughes, April Love,
oil on canvas, Tate
Gallery, bought by
Morris in 1856 on
Rossetti's advice.*

Both Burne-Jones and Morris fell under the spell of Rossetti's intense charm; vital, generous, witty, his essential instability not yet apparent, he was a man of great personal fascination. Only a few years their senior, he nevertheless enjoyed the adulation of his young disciples and persuaded Morris to take up painting rather than architecture. His influence was immense; 'I want to imitate Gabriel as much as I can', Morris told Burne-Jones. Rossetti encouraged Morris not only to take up painting but also to buy some of the work of his other friends; on his advice, Morris acquired *April Love*, a painting by Arthur Hughes, a young artist who had adopted the Pre-Raphaelite style.

This year also saw the beginnings of experiments in the applied arts. In November Morris and Burne-Jones moved from their lodgings in Upper Gordon Street to Rossetti's former rooms in Red Lion Square. According to Mackail, Morris was already at about this time modelling in clay, carving in wood and stone, and illuminating books. Their new rooms were unfurnished and Morris, unable to find a chair or table to his taste, had some made to his own specifications: 'table and chairs like incubi and succubi ... intensely mediaeval', wrote Rossetti to William Allingham, the poet. The settle was so enormous that when it arrived Morris and Burne-Jones came home to find that 'the passages and the staircase were choked with vast blocks of timber, and there was a scene. I think the measurements had perhaps been given a little wrongly, and that it was bigger altogether than he had ever meant, but set up it was finally, and our studio was one-third less in size'.

Morris's career as a painter was brief. Throughout his successful career as a designer he was never at ease with figurative work. The subject for his first oil painting, taken from Malory's *Morte d'Arthur*, was: *How Sir Tristram, After His Illness, Was Recognized by a little Dog He had Given to Iseult*. Morris and Burne-Jones had first discovered Malory in the form of Southey's 1816 reprint, which they found in a Birmingham bookshop in the summer of 1855. Written in the late 15th century and published by Caxton in 1485, Sir Thomas Malory's *Morte d'Arthur* was the last flowering of Arthurian legend in the literature of the Middle Ages. Morris and Burne-Jones found this work, with its nostalgic celebration of chivalric ideals and courtly love, deeply sympathetic: 'The book can never have been loved as it was by those two men', recalled Georgiana, Burne-Jones's wife. The Arthurian legends were not then well known, and Mackail records that they pair regarded the *Morte d'Arthur* as 'so precious that even among their intimates there was some shyness over it, till a year later they heard Rossetti speak of it and the Bible as the two greatest books in the world, and their tongues were unloosed by the sanction of his authority'.

In the summer of 1857 Morris left his painting unfinished and went to Oxford with Burne-Jones, in order to join Rossetti and other young artists in painting a series of murals on Arthurian subjects in the Oxford Union Society's Debating Hall (the present library). Rossetti was a friend of Benjamin Woodward, the architect of the Debating Hall, which he visited when it was newly completed in the Venetian Gothic style early in the summer of 1857. Rossetti offered to fill the bays between the windows with frescoes of scenes from Malory's *Morte d'Arthur* and to recruit a group of artists to do the work for nothing but their expenses. Rossetti, Morris and Burne-Jones arrived first and took rooms at 87 High Street, opposite Queen's College. They were joined by John Hungerford Pollen, Arthur Hughes, Val Prinsep and Roddam Spencer-Stanhope; of these only Hughes was Academy-trained (and Prinsep was only 19). It was an amateur undertaking, one embarked on with great exuberance and *joie de vivre*.

RIGHT *Morris's Oxford mural, Sir Palomydes's Jealousy of Sir Tristram, 1857. The story of Tristram and Iseult was a favourite of Morris's. Unfortunately the Oxford murals began to fade soon after they were completed because the walls were not prepared properly.*

For the Oxford Union, Morris again chose a subject from the story of Tristram and Iseult: *How Sir Palomides Loved La Belle Iseult with Exceeding Great Love out of Measure, and how She Loved Not Him Again but Rather Sir Tristram.* For Morris, practical and energetic but also highly emotional, the simplicity of the great love story and the character of Tristram – courageous and vigorous, a constant and passionate lover, a hunter and musician – were very attractive. Morris tackled his mural with typical energy; he was the first to begin and the first to finish. Unfortunately, the walls were not properly prepared and almost immediately the murals, at first 'so brilliant as to make the walls look like the margin of an illuminated manuscript' in the words of the poet Coventry Patmore, began to disappear. Morris's was one of the worst affected and little now remains. He went on to decorate the ceiling with a convoluted design of leaves and flowers, which prefigures his later decorative work. The width of his range of interests and his eagerness to tackle and to master new crafts were now becoming evident. Burne-Jones recalled:

*For the purposes of our drawing we often needed armour, and of a date and design so remote that no examples existed for our use. Therefore Morris, whose knowledge of these things seemed to have been born in him, and who never at any time needed books of reference for anything, set to work to make designs for an ancient kind of helmet called a basinet, and for a great surcoat of ringed mail with a hood of mail and the skirt coming below the knees. These were made for him by a stout little smith who had a forge near the Castle. Morris's visits to the forge were daily, but what scenes happened there we shall never know; the encounters between these two workmen were always stubborn and angry as far as I could see. One afternoon when I was working high up at my picture, I heard a strange bellowing in the building, and turning round to find the cause, saw an unwonted sight. The basinet was being tried on, but the visor, for some reason, would not lift, and I saw Morris embedded in iron, dancing with rage and roaring inside. The mail coat came in due time, and was so satisfactory to its designer that the first day it came he chose to dine in it. It became him well; he looked very splended.*

RIGHT *The Oxford Union Library, designed by Benjamin Woodward, with murals by Rossetti, Prinsep and Pollen. The ceiling decoration was designed by Morris.*

These were not Morris's only attempts about this time to design the costumes which he and Burne-Jones needed for their medieval subjects. The William Morris Gallery owns two

RIGHT *Rossetti's Oxford mural, Sir Launcelot's Vision of the Sanc Grail. Burne-Jones was the model for the figure of Launcelot, Jane Burden, later Morris's wife, for Guinevere, and Elizabeth Siddal, later Rossetti's wife, for the Grail angel.*

LEFT *Valentine Prinsep, Sir Pelleas Leaving the Lady Ettard, mural, Oxford Union Library.*

LEFT *John Roddam Spencer-Stanhope*, Sir Gawaine Meeting Three Ladies at the Well, *mural, Oxford Union Library*.

RIGHT *Edward Burne-Jones*, Merlin and Nimue, *mural, Oxford Union Library*.

RIGHT *Arthur Hughes*, Arthur Carried Away to Avalon and the Sword Thrown back into the Lake, *mural, Oxford Union Library*.

costumes designed by Morris around 1857, both in a quasi-medieval style: one is a dress in pink wool, the other a sideless gown with a full skirt in white cotton.

This was a carefree period in Morris's life; the work in the Oxford Union went on in an atmosphere of uproarious laughter and practical joking, of which Morris, with his quick temper, was often the butt. One undergraduate who came to watch the work in progress and stayed to become a friend was Algernon Swinburne, the poet, then a student at Balliol. A favourite topic of conversation was, not unnaturally, attractive young women, or 'stunners', as they were known in Rossettian slang. The group of high-spirited young men rather enjoyed shocking casual visitors to the Oxford Union. Swinburne gleefully recounted one such incident in a letter to a friend:

*One evening when the Union was just finished, Jones and I had a great talk. Stanhope and Swan attacked, and we defended, our idea of Heaven, viz. a rose-garden full of stunners. Atrocities of an appalling nature were uttered on the other side. We became so fierce that two respectable members of the University – entering to see the pictures – stood mute and looked at us. We spoke just then of kisses in Paradise, and expounded our ideas on the celestial development of that necessity of life; and after listening five minutes to our language, they literally fled from the room! Conceive our mutual ecstasy of delight.*

Rossetti was constantly on the lookout for 'stunners' to act as artist's models, and this preoccupation was to have far-reaching consequences for Morris during this summer in Oxford. There is some uncertainty about how Rossetti met Jane Burden, Morris's future wife, but according to Mackail he and Burne-Jones saw her at the theatre in Oxford towards the end of the long vacation. Rossetti was struck by her extraordinary looks and asked her to model for the group. Probably Rossetti himself was much attracted to her – certainly he was later to fall deeply in love with her – but he was at that time emotionally committed to another young woman, Elizabeth Siddall. This involvement, although not very happy, was to lead to marriage in 1860. Recent writers have thought it likely that Jane fell in love with Rossetti at this time; nevertheless, when Morris fell in love with her and proposed, she accepted, and they became engaged in the spring of 1858. Even if she had not been in love with Morris, his offer would have been extremely difficult to refuse. Although abrupt and rough in manner, he was rich, good-natured and not unattractive. Jane, the daughter of an ostler, came from a humble working-class background, and marriage to a gentleman was probably her only chance of bettering herself.

Morris had finished his work in the Oxford Union by the end of November, but stayed on in lodgings at 17 George Street, working on the oil painting which he had begun earlier in the year. One other painting, La Belle Iseult, for which the model was Jane Burden, was tackled and completed before he abandoned painting. *La Belle Iseult* (now in the Tate Gallery, London), with its attention to pattern, fabric and costume, shows that even in painting a picture, Morris's deep interest in decorative art was paramount. The splendour of Iseult's dress tends to direct the spectator's attention away from the deficiencies of the figure drawing. According to one of Morris's biographers,

LEFT *Portrait of Swinburne by William Bell Scott, oil on canvas, 1860, Balliol College, Oxford.*

RIGHT Morris's only
surviving oil painting,
La Belle Iseult,
1858, now in the Tate
Gallery, in London.
The subject is from
Arthurian legend, and
the model was Jane
Burden, who became
Morris's wife in 1859.

LEFT *Caricature by Rossetti*, Morris presenting an Engagement Ring to Jane, *Birmingham City Museums and Art Gallery*.

Gerald Crow, Morris was said to have written, 'I cannot paint you but I love you' on a drawing of Jane as Iseult.

Morris's interest in Arthurian legend was finding literary as well as visual expression in these years. While at work on his murals he produced what are now usually considered some of his best poems in *The Defence of Guenevere and Other Poems*, published in March 1858 and dedicated 'To my friend, Dante Gabriel Rossetti, Painter'. The verses in this book, wholly on medieval themes, are varied in tone, some arcane and illusive, others relating dramatic, often violent, episodes with an intense and vividly realistic use of language. This was a volume of extraordinarily forceful and original poetry, but such critical notice as there was tended to be disparaging. Morris wrote nothing like it again.

On 26 April 1859 William and Jane were married at St Michael's parish church in Oxford. At least one of Morris's friends thought that they were an incongruous pair: Swinburne wrote to a friend that he liked to think of Morris 'having that wonderful and most perfect stunner of his to – look at or speak to. The idea of his marrying her is insane. To kiss her feet is the utmost man should dream of doing'.

CHAPTER TWO

# THE FIRM

'Daisy', 1862,
Morris's second
wallpaper design, the
first to be printed in
1864. It was based on
a wall-hanging which
Morris designed for
Red House.

RIGHT *Red House,*
1859, *designed by*
*Philip Webb and built*
*for Morris at Bexley*
*Heath, Kent.*

IN SPITE OF SWINBURNE'S reservations, the early years of Morris's marriage were happy. He and his wife began their married life in Red House at Bexleyheath in Kent, designed for them by Philip Webb, who had just left Street's practice to set up on his own as an architect. This charming and unpretentious house is a good early example of the neo-vernacular Gothic style, which was already being used by Street and William Butterfield, another Gothic Revival architect whose work Webb admired, for domestic buildings, particularly vicarages. Red House derived its name from the local brick in which it was built and was situated in an orchard; Mackail notes that 'the building had been planned with such care that hardly a tree ... had to be cut down; apples fell in at the windows as they stood open on hot autumn nights'. It was built in the form of an L-shape with a turreted well, which supplied their water, in the angle. A rose trellis formed the other two sides of the square.

LEFT A *doorway of*
Red House, *showing*
*the beautiful warm*
*colour of the local brick*
*after which it was*
*named.*

LEFT *The front entrance of Red House.*

Morris had wanted 'a house very mediaeval in spirit': the house with its irregular skyline, hipped and gabled roofs, and small-paned windows is perhaps more romantic and picturesque than genuinely medieval in design and style.

In 1860 Rossetti married Elizabeth Siddall, and Burne-Jones, Georgiana Macdonald. Red House, in the middle of the fertile Kentish countryside, three miles from the nearest station, was a weekend retreat for both the young married couples and for Morris's other friends, among them Webb, Faulkner and his sisters, Kate and Lucy, Arthur Hughes and Swinburne. Morris kept open house: 'it was a home of young people full of the high spirits of youth', as Mackail records. Practical jokes abounded, usually with Morris, who was very susceptible to teasing, as the victim. WR Lethaby's biography of Philip Webb records some amusing incidents: 'When playing whist, Burne-Jones and Faulkner arranged a pack of cards so that

Morris had a hand over which he beamed, but he lost everything, and flung his cards down. "You fellows have been at it again". Another time they "took in" and sewed up Morris's waistcoat and charged him with getting even abnormally fat'. Another friend recalled that 'it was the most beautiful sight in the world . . . to see Morris coming up from the cellar before dinner, beaming with joy, with his hands full of bottles of wine and others tucked under his arms'. Two tragedies marred these years: the birth of a stillborn child to Rossetti's wife in 1861 and her death from an overdose of laudanum in the following year. For Morris, however, the years at Red House were probably the happiest of his life; here his two daughters were born, in 1861 Jane Alice, always known as Jenny to distinguish her from her mother, and in 1862 Mary, always known as May.

As with the rooms in Red Lion Square, Morris's dissatisfaction with contemporary

RIGHT St. Matthew, *designed by Morris, 1862, Christchurch, Southgate, Middlesex.*

LEFT The Sermon on the Mount, *stained glass designed by Rossetti, 1862, All Saints, Selsley, Gloucestershire.*

furnishings led him to design, or to encourage others to design, furniture and other household goods more suitable for his new house. As Mackail describes it:

> . . . only in a few isolated cases – such as Persian carpets, and blue china or delft for vessels of household use – was there anything then to be bought ready-made that Morris could be content with in his own house. Not a chair, a table, or a bed; not a cloth or paper hanging for the walls; nor tiles to line fireplaces or passages; nor a jug to hold wine or a glass to drink it out of, but had to be reinvented, one might almost say, to escape the flat ugliness of the current article. The great painted settle from Red Lion Square was taken and set up in the drawing-room, the top of it being railed in so as to form a small music gallery. Much of the furniture was specially designed by Webb and executed under his eye: the great oak dining-table, other tables, chairs, cupboards, massive copper candlesticks, firedogs, and table glass of extreme beauty.

The decoration of Red House was a truly communal effort. Burne-Jones painted the drawing-room walls with scenes from the medieval romance of *Sire Degrevaunt* and designed painted tiles for the fireplaces. Other walls were covered in hangings designed by Morris and worked by Jane and by Elizabeth Siddall. Rossetti painted a scene from Dante's *Vita Nuova* on the doors of the settle. It was this work on Red House which led in 1861 to the idea of setting up a firm to do similar work on a commercial basis. As Rossetti later described it to his friend Theodore Watts-Dunton, the beginnings of the firm of Morris, Marshall, Faulkner and Company were extremely informal: 'One evening, a lot of us were together, and we got talking about the way in which artists did all kinds of things in olden times, designed every kind of decoration and most kinds of furniture, and someone suggested –

LEFT St Peter and St Paul, *designed by Morris and Ford Madox Brown*, 1865, Middleton Cheney, Northamptonshire.

RIGHT The Brachet Licking Sir Tristram *designed by Morris, 1861, one of a series of stained glass panels illustrating the story of Sir Tristram, made in 1862 for Harden Grange, near Bingley, West Yorkshire, the home of Walter Dunlop, a Bradford merchant.*

How Sir Tristram slew a giant who would have slain King Mark and how King Mark not knowing him brought him to Tintagel, and how he got his wit again and how Isoude knew him again by cause of the brachet which Tristram had given her which leaped upon him and licked him

as a joke more than anything else – that we should each put down five pounds and form a company'. According to Mackail, 'the Firm', as it became known, was begun even more modestly on £1 shares and an unsecured loan of £100 from Morris's mother. Lack of capital was always a problem in the early years.

As well as Rossetti, the Firm's founding members included Burne-Jones and Ford Madox Brown (1821–93), an associate of the early days of the Pre-Raphaelites; both had experience in stained-glass design. Webb of course was a member, and Faulkner, who had held a mathematics tutorship at Oxford, looked after the accounts. Marshall, who in fact played little part in the Firm, was a surveyor and sanitary engineer, a friend of Ford Madox Brown. Premises consisting of the first and third floors were taken at 8 Red Lion Square; a kiln for firing tiles and glass was built in the basement.

Morris expected that much of the Firm's work would be ecclesiastical, and it was. The tremendous and continuing urban expansion of the first half of the century had led to an increase in church-building, and the rise of Anglo-Catholicism, with its emphasis on ceremony, the sacraments and church adornment, had created a healthy market for stained glass, tiles and all kinds of ecclesiastical furnishings. The Firm's prospectus, published in April 1861, claimed that 'the growth of Decorative Art in this country, owing to the efforts of English Architects, has now reached a point at which it seems desirable that Artists of repute should devote their time to it'. As Morris explained in a letter to his old tutor, the Reverend Guy, 'you see we are, or consider ourselves to be, the only really artistic firm of the kind'.

Morris was much influenced by the art critic John Ruskin (1819–1900), who felt that the growth of mass-production had debased the applied arts and degraded the craftsman; this message was eagerly absorbed by Morris and Burne-Jones from their reading of *The Stones of Venice* (1851–53), particularly the chapter entitled 'The Nature of Gothic', which they read at Oxford. Here Ruskin laid down the aesthetic and moral justification for preferring handicraft to mass-produced decoration: 'We have much studied and much perfected, of late, the great civilised invention of the division of labour; only we give it a false name. It is not, truly speaking, the labour that is divided; but the men ...'. Ruskin contrasted the spiritual deadness of perfectly finished machine-made goods, which reduced their makers to slaves, and the imperfect but more satisfying work of the craftsman. He held up the Middle Ages as an exemplar: 'In the mediaeval, or especially Christian, system of ornament, the slavery is done away with altogether; Christianity having recognised, in small things as well as great,

the individual value of every soul'. Looking around for furniture for his new house, Morris had seen for himself the ugliness or dullness of much mid-Victorian design. In the work of the Firm he wanted the eye and hand of the artist to be as evident in the finished object as in the original design.

The Firm began well by winning two medals for their exhibits in the Mediaeval Court of the 1862 International Exhibition, held at the South Kensington Museum (later the Victoria and Albert Museum), and by selling nearly £150 worth of goods there. So successfully did the Firm's stained glass emulate the skill and the spirit of medieval work that there were calls for it to be disqualified from the competition because it was thought to be medieval glass touched up. One much-admired exhibit, Rossetti's seven stained-glass panels of *The Parable of the Vineyard*, led to the Firm's first commissions for three new churches designed by the Gothic Revival architect, George Frederick Bodley: St Michael's in Brighton, St Martin's in Scarborough and All Saints, Selsley, Gloucestershire, all dating from 1862.

The Firm's work was part of a general revival of medieval techniques which had fallen into disuse since the Reformation, besides being a natural development of the Gothic Revival in church architecture. Stained glass of the 17th and 18th centuries is little more than pictures painted on glass; it fails to exploit the particular qualities of the medium. The intent of the medieval technique was to build as good a picture as possible with different coloured glass. The rich, glowing colour of medieval glass was also emulated. Most of the Firm's best stained glass was produced in the 1860s, probably because Morris supervised the manufacture with an attention for which he did not later have time. Burne-Jones was always his most prolific designer. In the early days designs were also contributed by Ford Madox Brown. In spite of his difficulty with figure

RIGHT *Wardrobe designed by Webb and painted by Burne-Jones with a subject from Chaucer's 'Prioresses's Tale', Ashmolean Museum. The portrait of Chaucer in the lower right hand corner was copied from a medieval manuscript.*

drawing, Morris designed some successful windows in the 1860s, notably an Annunciation for All Saints, Selsley, and a St Peter for All Saints, Cambridge, in 1866. Also of particular interest are four panels which he designed in 1862 as part of a series of 13 panels illustrating the story of Tristram, these for Harden Grange, near Bingley, West Yorkshire, the home of Walter Dunlop, a Bradford merchant. One of

these, *The Brachet Licking Sir Tristram*, showing Tristram recognized by the dog he had given to Iseult, is on the same subject as his first oil painting and might even be the same design.

Morris's initial wallpaper designs date from the early years of the Firm. 'Trellis', the first, was supposedly inspired by the garden at Red House; the birds were drawn by Philip Webb. This was followed by 'Daisy', based on

LEFT *Oak cabinet designed by J P Seddon in 1862 to hold his architectural drawings, decorated with scenes from the honeymoon of King Rene of Anjou by Madox Brown, Burne-Jones, Morris and Rossetti.*

a wall-hanging designed by Morris for Red House, and 'Fruit', or 'Pomegranate'. Although they were designed in 1862, the wallpapers were not produced until 1864–66. These designs, with their fresh, almost naïve charm, were less popular in the 1860s than they are today; they were counter to the current taste for hothouse flowers and did not sell well. Morris designed no more until the 1870s. This was an area in which Morris did not adhere to the principle of having everything designed by the Firm manufactured by the Firm; wallpapers were sent out to the firm of Jeffrey and Company in Islington to be hand-printed from blocks. This work, although skilled, allowed for little individual contribution from the workman. Later on, many carpets, chintzes and silks were also made outside the Firm. Nor was Morris always averse to the use of machinery if this could make a laborious job less tedious. George Bernard Shaw remembered visiting Morris's Merton Abbey works and daring to say of some process, 'You should get a machine

to do that'. Morris replied, 'I've ordered one'.

One process which remained pre-industrial in technique was the Firm's embroidery. Embroidery was an interest which Morris shared with Jane, who was an excellent needle-woman. After their marriage he taught her medieval embroidery techniques; after Morris's death she recalled their early experiments and how she made the 'Daisy' hanging for Red House:

> . . . we studied old pieces, and by unpicking etc, we learnt much, but it was uphill work, fascinating but only carried on through his enormous energy and perseverance . . . the first stuff I got to embroider on was a piece of indigo-dyed blue serge I found by chance in a London shop . . . I took it home and he was delighted with it and set to work at once designing flowers. These we worked in bright colour in a rough simple way. The work went quickly and when finished we covered the walls of the bedroom at Red House to our great joy.

The Firm's first embroideries were worked by Jane, her sister Bessie, Georgiana Burne-Jones, Mrs George Campbell (the wife of the

RIGHT 'Morris' adjustable-back oak armchair, adapted by Webb from a Sussex type at the suggestion of Warrington Taylor, the Firm's business manager, in about 1866. It is covered in 'Vine', a woven woollen cloth designed by Dearle, c. 1890; he designed many of the Firm's later textiles, such as the one on the opposite page, 'Michaelmas Daisy', first produced in 1912.

LEFT 'Sussex' chair, a
rush-seated armchair
of ebonized beechwood
adapted by Webb
from a traditional
model. This popular
design continued in
production for nearly
eighty years.

company foreman), and Faulkner's two sisters, Lucy and Kate. As with stained glass, many of the Firm's early commissions were ecclesiastical; the work on Bodley's new churches in 1862, for example, included altar frontals and other church embroidery, which were designed by Morris and Webb.

Webb took a major part in the Firm's early work; most of the furniture was designed by him, with contributions by Ford Madox Brown. Morris designed no more after the days in Red Lion Square. The furniture made by the Firm was basically of two kinds, although simplicity of design, robustness and honesty of construction were the characteristics of both. The first was the kind of furniture which had been created for Red House – massive, medieval in spirit and specifically designed to be painted. Such furniture was of necessity expensive and could be produced only in limited numbers. The second, and more popular, type of furniture was based on traditional models; the

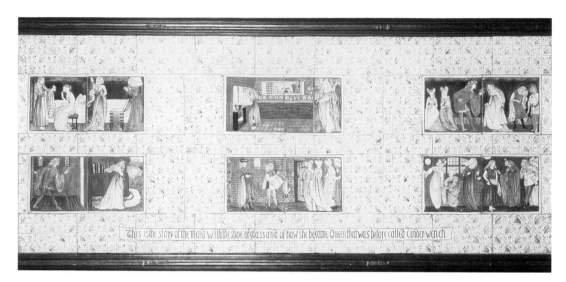

LEFT *Tile panel illustrating the story of Cinderella, designed by Burne-Jones and Webb, painted by Lucy Faulkner for the house of the Victorian watercolourist, Miles Birket Foster, 1863.*

RIGHT *'September'. Detail from the fireplace tile panel at Queen's College Hall, Cambridge.*

'Sussex' chair, for example, a rush-seated armchair of ebonized beechwood, was adapted by Webb from a Sussex design and sold in large numbers, continuing in production for nearly 80 years.

Hand-painted tiles were among the earliest products of the Firm. Morris did not make his own tiles, but bought factory-made blanks in large quantities, these being painted and then fired in the kiln at Red Lion Square. Mackail records that although members of the Firm – Rossetti, Burne-Jones, Webb and Morris – contributed most of the designs, 'other artists, including Albert Moore, William De Morgan [later to be a highly successful potter in his own right], and Simeon Solomon, made occasional designs for glass and tiles; and as in the days of the Union paintings, every one who could be got hold of was expected to bear a hand'. The results were often delightfully lively, due to Morris's insistence on hand-painting; of particular charm are the Beauty and the Beast panel, designed by Burne-Jones and painted by Lucy Faulkner, and the fireplace tile panel depicting the Seasons and other figures in Queen's College Hall, Cambridge, which had been restored by Bodley.

The Firm also supplied jewellery and glass-

LEFT *Tile panel designed by Burne-Jones, probably painted by Lucy or Kate Faulkner, around 1861.*

RIGHT *The Virgin Mary, from the fireplace tile panel at Queen's College Hall, Cambridge.*

LEFT *Saint Bernard, from the fireplace tile panel at Queen's College Hall, Cambridge.*

ware, again with Webb as the designer. There was no pandering to public taste, and Morris's way of doing business was unconventional; customers were surprised to find him serving in the shop himself. Mackail records one such visit:

> 'I perfectly remember', writes Mrs Richmond Ritchie of a visit to Red Lion Square early in 1862, 'going with Val Prinsep one foggy morning to some square, miles away; we came into an empty ground floor room, and Val Prinsep called "Topsy" [Morris's nickname, taken from Uncle Tom's Cabin] very loud, and some one came from above with hair on end and in a nonchalant way began to show one or two of his curious, and to my uninitiated soul, bewildering treasures. I think Morris said that the glasses would stand firm when he put them on the table. I bought two tumblers of which Val Prinsep praised the shape. He and Val wrapped them up in paper, and I came away very much amused and interested, with a general impression of sympathetic shyness and shadows and dim green glass'.

The great happiness of Morris's convivial years at Red House, which were enlivened by the constant visits of his friends, led him to plan the establishment of a permanent artistic community there. As the workload of the Firm increased it seemed, too, that it might be a more practical arrangement to move the works out to Kent and establish a factory there. In addition to this, in 1864 Morris was hoping to add another wing to Red House to accommodate Edward Burne-Jones and his wife and family. Unfortunately, this plan foundered. Georgiana Burne-Jones became seriously ill with scarlet fever and because of this Burne-Jones felt that it would be more prudent to remain in London. This grieved Morris, who was ill himself with rheumatic fever at the time; a letter written in a shaky hand reveals his emotional nature, which at ordinary times he kept under a tight control; the letter also reveals his love of his closest friend:

LEFT *Fireplace tile panel depicting seasons and saints, Queen's College Hall, Cambridge, 1862–4, designed by Burne-Jones, Morris, Rossetti, and Ford Madox Brown.*

*. . . as to our palace of Art, I confess your letter was a blow to me at first, though hardly an unexpected one – in short I cried; but I have got over it now. . . . I refuse to make myself really unhappy for anything short of the loss of friends one can't do without. Suppose in all these troubles you had given us the slip what the devil should I have done? I am sure I couldn't have had the heart to go on with the firm . . .'*

This was the end of Morris's happy life at Red House. He was not really well enough after his recovery from rheumatic fever to travel daily to London, and the Firm was not doing sufficiently well for a move out to Kent to be feasible. At the same time Morris's private income was affected by a decline in the value of his inherited copper shares; with great reluctance he decided that he would have to move to London.

New premises were leased by the Firm from summer 1865; Morris and his family were to live above the shop. In autumn of that year they left Red House. Some of the furniture was too heavy to be moved and in any case had

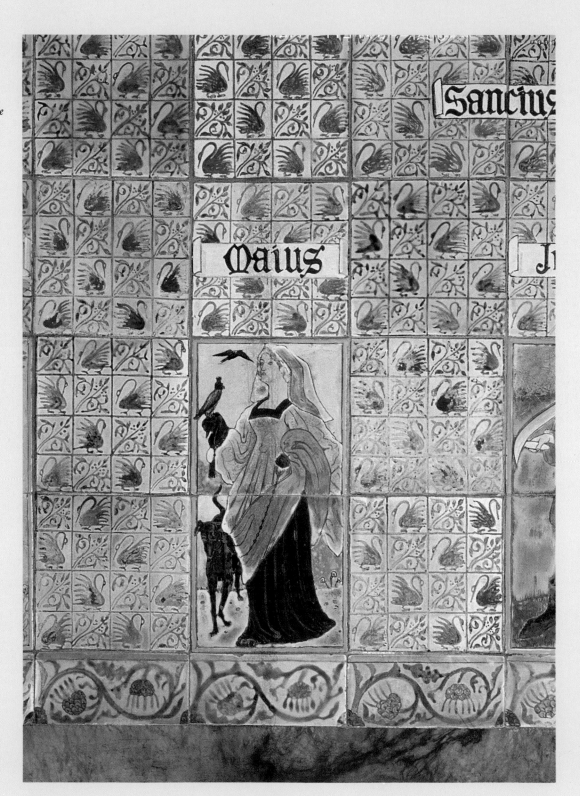

RIGHT May, from the
fireplace tile panel.

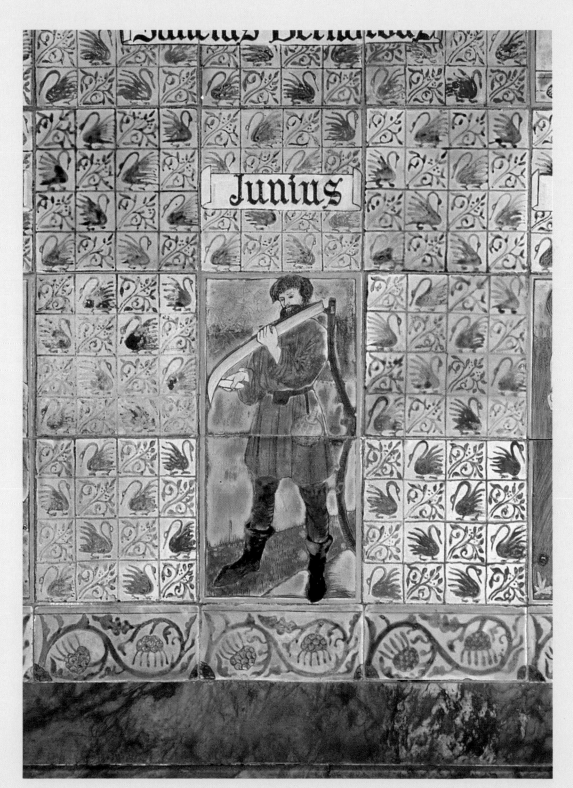

LEFT June, from the
fireplace tile panel.

RIGHT Archangels, Raphael, Michael, and Gabriel, *stained glass designed by Morris, 1869, St Mary, Kings Walden, Hertfordshire.*

LEFT *Detail of angels, designed by Morris, 1873, St Peter and St Paul, Over Stowey, Somerset.*

RIGHT *Queen Square, Bloomsbury, a print of around 1820. Morris and his family moved to No. 26 in 1865. The Firm's office and showroom was on the first floor and a large ballroom behind the house was turned into a workshop.*

been specifically designed for rooms in Red House; it was impossible to move Burne-Jones's murals. The abandonment of this beloved home was a great sorrow to Morris; he never saw it again, feeling, Mackail says, that 'the sight of it would be more than he could bear'. Morris's new home at 26 Queen Square was a spacious Queen Anne building in Bloomsbury. The ground floor was turned into an office and showroom, and a large ballroom behind the house became a workshop.

The necessity of leaving Red House had shown how essential it was that the Firm's finances be put in order. Faulkner's return to Oxford in 1864 was now allowing him much less time to look after the books. He was succeeded by Warrington Taylor, who was the Firm's business manager from 1865 until his early death from consumption in 1870 (according to Lethaby he was only 34). Taylor was horrified by the chaotic way in which the business was run and his reforms, carried out

almost in the teeth of Morris, were responsible for giving the Firm a sound economic base from which it could develop. For the sake of his health, Taylor moved to Hastings soon after his appointment and carried on much of his work with the Firm by letter; some of these missives give a very vivid picture of Morris's unbusiness-like habits and also of his way of living. In 1869 Taylor wrote to Morris:

> *It's no good your screaming and saying you will shut the bloody shop up. You can't afford to do it any longer . . .. It is evident that you must give up entertaining. You have not the means to do it. . . . It's no good your blasting anybody's eyes – you must haul in. . . . How can any man dream of entertaining and going out on £700 a year on which he pays £100 for rent and taxes nearly. You must reduce your wine consumption down to 2½ bottles a day – this at 1/6 is somewhere about £68 a year.*

He was equally frank about Morris's poor

organization of the Firm, writing this in a letter to Rossetti:

> Morris is often very nervous about work, and consequently often suddenly takes men off one job and puts them onto another. There is in this great loss of time. . . . Morris will start half a dozen jobs; he has only designs for perhaps half of them, and therefore in a week or two they have to be given up. They are put away, bits get lost, have to be done over again: Hence great loss of time and money'.

By the time of his death Taylor had managed with difficulty to train Morris into more business-like ways.

Two important decorative schemes in the second half of the 1860s greatly increased the Firm's reputation. These were the commissions to decorate the Armoury and Tapestry Rooms at St James's Palace and the Green Dining Room for the South Kensington Museum, now the Victoria and Albert Museum, both designed by Webb in 1866. In addition to these two public commissions, much fine church decoration was carried out, one notable example being the restored Jesus College Chapel in Cambridge, on which the Firm began work in 1866.

As he was spared the daily journey in and out of London, the move to Queen Square gave Morris more time to devote to other pursuits, and he began work on a cycle of narrative poems which had been planned at Red House. This was The Earthly Paradise, which Morris intended to publish with woodcuts by Burne-Jones, a project which was never realized. The Earthly Paradise, set in the 14th century, tells the story of men who flee the Black Death and set sail to find the Earthly Paradise. They reach a western island inhabited by a race descended from the ancient Greeks; here Greek and northern European cultures mingle. Each month for a year the travellers, variously of Norse, Breton and Germanic origin, entertain their hosts with a story and in

turn are told a story by them. These 24 stories form the body of The Earthly Paradise and are retellings of stories from various sources: Greek mythology, French and German romances, Norse and Icelandic sagas. Chaucer's Canterbury Tales and Boccaccio's The Decameron both have a similar framework, and indeed Morris admitted to using Chaucer as his model for The Earthly Paradise. Morris wrote at great speed, working at night and early in the morning, sometimes producing as much as 700 lines a day; in all The Earthly Paradise was 42,000 words long. One story, The Life and Death of Jason, grew so long that it was published separately in 1867. Critical acclaim was far warmer than it had been for The Defence of Guenevere, and the poem achieved immediate popular success; encouraged by this, Morris published the first volume of The Earthly Paradise in 1868. Volumes II and III were published in 1870. The poem established Morris's reputation; indeed he was far better known as a poet than as a designer during his lifetime. Much of the attraction of The Earthly Paradise lay in its undemanding readability; unlike Morris's early poetry, it was accessible to the ordinary mid-Victorian reader. The drama, abrupt rhythms, sensuality and violence of his early poetry were replaced by soothing cadences, a leisurely narrative pace and bowdlerized material. So soothing was it that Georgiana Burne-Jones, to whom Morris read his poetry aloud, remembered with shame 'often falling asleep to the steady rhythm of the reading voice, or biting my fingers and stabbing myself with pins to keep awake'.

In 1870 Morris was 36 and at the height of his reputation as a poet. In the nine years since its inception the Firm, of which he was the manager and leading partner, had produced some of the finest stained glass of the 19th century and was now a well-established supplier of the decorative arts. Ahead lay busy and successful years in which Morris

RIGHT *Chalk drawing of Jenny, Morris's elder daughter, by Rossetti, Kelmscott Manor, 1871. She was diagnosed as an epileptic at the age of fifteen and from then on lived as an invalid.*

LEFT *Chalk drawing of Morris's second daughter, May, by Rossetti, Kelmscott Manor, 1871. May shared her father's commitment to socialism and was a professional embroidress. From 1885 she managed this aspect of the Firm's work.*

RIGHT The Green
Dining-room,
designed by Webb for
the Victoria and
Albert Museum,
1866. The window
and painted wall
panels are by Burne-
Jones, the walls, with
raised gesso
decoration, frieze and
ceiling, by Webb.

would extend his skills to textile design and eventually to typography; throughout he would continue his writing. The next decade or so would see an increasing involvement in public affairs, culminating in a passionate commitment to socialism.

To outward appearance, Morris was a successful man with a settled family life and an abundance of friends. Yet these middle years were the most unhappy of Morris's life. Mackail writes that in the verses that frame the stories of *The Earthly Paradise* 'there is an autobiography so delicate and so outspoken that it must needs be left to speak for itself'. Writing when Morris's wife and daughters were still alive, Mackail could not be much more specific; he confided to a friend the difficulties caused by 'the constant need for what is called "tact", which is a quality unpleasantly near untruthfulness often'. In the years after the move from Red House in 1865 the happiness of Morris's married life was over; he became increasingly aware that his marriage had failed. His wife was in love with another man.

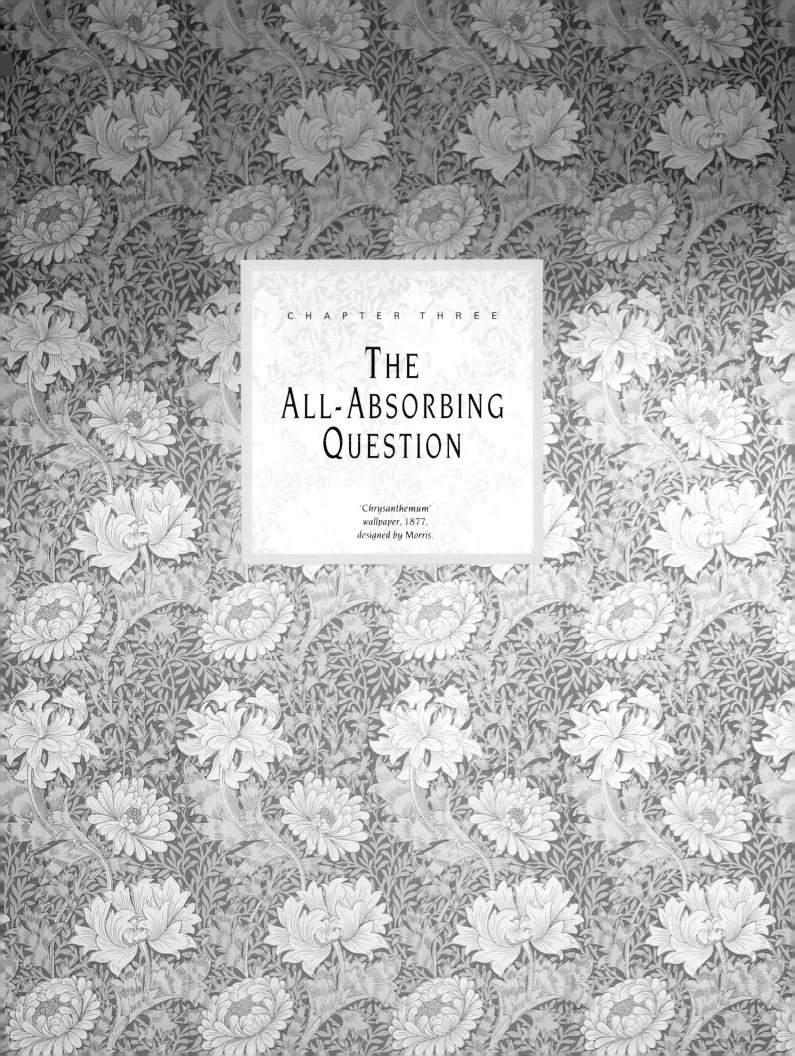

CHAPTER THREE

# THE
# ALL-ABSORBING
# QUESTION

*'Chrysanthemum'*
*wallpaper, 1877,*
*designed by Morris.*

RIGHT *Photograph of
Jane Morris posed by
Rossetti in the garden
of his house at
Cheyne Walk in
1865.*

LEFT *Photograph of
Rossetti by Lewis
Carroll, 1863.*

*Imagine a tall lean woman in a long dress of some
dead purple stuff, guiltless of hoops . . . with a mass
of crisp black hair heaped into great wavy
projections on each side of her temples, a thin pale
face, a pair of strange sad, deep, dark, Swinburnian
eyes, with great thick black oblique brows, joined in
the middle of and tucking themselves away under
her hair . . . a long neck, without any collar, and in
lieu thereof some dozen strings of outlandish beads.
On the wall was a large nearly full-length portrait
of her by Rossetti . . .*

THIS MARVELLOUS DESCRIPTION of Jane
Morris is from a letter which Henry James, the
American novelist, wrote to his sister in March
1869, describing an evening spent with Morris
and his wife. Jane had a toothache and lay on
the sofa after dinner with a handkerchief over
her face, while Morris read from the second
volume of *The Earthly Paradise*: 'There was
something very quaint and remote from our
actual life, it seemed to me, in the whole
scene: Morris reading in his flowing antique
numbers a legend of prodigies and terrors . . .
around us all the picturesque bric-a-brac of
the apartment . . . and in the corner this dark
silent medieval woman with her medieval

toothache'. Jane is an enigmatic figure here
and to some extent that is how she has remained. Sydney Cockerell, Morris's secretary
in the last years of his life, admitted in his
introduction to Mackail's biography of Morris
that Jane could seem to some people 'awe-
inspiring and unapproachable', but added that
'she had a charming unaffected nature, and
was as responsive to fun as any child'. Georgiana Burne-Jones's description of her playing
hide-and-seek at Red House seems to bear
this out.

The first years of her marriage seem to have
been at least contented, even if she was not
deeply in love with Morris. Even so he could
not have been an easy man with whom to
live. His energy and restlessness would erupt
into sudden uncontrollable rages, possibly
epileptic in origin, for which he was famous
among his friends. There are stories of him
kicking through the panel of a door if the knob
did not turn immediately in his hand and of
throwing his dinner out of the window. His
contempt for conventional manners and his
unkempt appearance – Henry James described

LEFT *Rossetti,*
*Mariana, 1868–*
*1870, oil on canvas,*
*now in the Aberdeen*
*Art Gallery and*
*Museums. The subject*
*is from Shakespeare's*
Measure for
Measure *and shows*
*Mariana pining for*
*the lover who has*
*jilted her. The model*
*is Jane Morris.*

him as 'corpulent, very careless and unfinished in his dress' – might have been irksome to Jane, who presumably did not have Morris's social confidence. In about 1865, after the move to Queen Square, Jane began to grow closer to Rossetti, with whom she later admitted to having been very much in love; Morris's affection for her remained unaltered.

In 1862 Rossetti had moved to 16 Cheyne Walk in Chelsea. He was suffering great grief

RIGHT *Rossetti,* Proserpine, *oil on canvas, Birmingham Museum and Art Gallery, 1882 (a version of a picture first painted in 1872). One of many for which Jane Morris was the model, it shows Proserpine condemned to remain in Hades with her husband, Pluto, for part of the year after eating a pomegranate. A reference to Jane's marriage to Morris may be intended.*

and guilt over the death of his wife, who had probably committed suicide. In the summer of 1865 Jane posed for Rossetti for a series of drawings, the first of many to be produced over the next few years. At the same time Rossetti had a series of photographs taken of her which reveal her extraordinary melancholy beauty. Over the next few years Jane was often at Cheyne Walk and in 1868 corresponded secretly with Rossetti while she was on holiday with Morris. Rossetti's devotion to her was becoming obvious. At one party he was observed feeding her strawberries, oblivious to the other guests; of his behaviour at another, his friend, William Bell Scott, observed that Rossetti 'acts like a perfect fool if he wants to conceal his attachment, doing nothing but attend to her, sitting sideways towards her, that sort of thing'.

The emotional strain was detrimental to the health of both the lovers. The beginnings of Rossetti's slow decline through drugs and drink can be dated from this period. His way of living, always Bohemian, became increasingly irregular. By 1869 Jane had succumbed to an illness which was never really diagnosed and may have been psychosomatic. In the summer Morris took her to Bad Ems, a spa in Germany, where it was hoped that taking the waters would benefit her. Rossetti suffered much in her absence and wrote to her with passionate longing: 'All that concerns you is the all-absorbing question with me'. The letters continued on Jane's return, Rossetti writing in February of the following year, 'To be with you and wait on you and read to you is absolutely the only happiness I can find or conceive in this world, dearest Janey'. Shortly after this Jane spent a month alone with him in a cottage in Sussex. Scandal was avoided only by Morris's acceptance of the situation and by the discretion of their immediate circle. Divorce would have been socially ruinous for Jane and does not even seem to have been

LEFT '*Missing*', *a poem from* A Book of Verse, *written and illuminated by Morris in 1870 for Georgiana Burne-Jones on her thirtieth birthday.*

contemplated. In 1871 it became possible for the lovers to spend more time together, when Rossetti and Morris took on the joint lease of Kelmscott Manor in Gloucestershire.

Morris by now had achieved some sort of accommodation of the situation, but this acceptance had not been reached without a long and painful struggle. Not surprisingly, added to the loss of his wife's affection was the gradual loss of the friendship of Rossetti, whom he had so revered. Morris's poetry of these years often seems to allude to the situation he was in, and in the lines on September in *The Earthly Paradise* Morris writes:

*Look long, O longing eyes, and look in vain!*
*Strain idly, aching heart, and yet be wise,*
*And hope no more for things to come again*
*That thou beheldest once with careless eyes!*
*Like a new-awakened man thou art, who tries*
*To dream again the dream that made him glad*
*When in his arms his loving love he had.*

RIGHT *Photograph by Hollyer of the Morris and Burne-Jones families in the garden of Burne-Jones's house, The Grange, in Fulham, 1874. From left to right are Georgiana Burne-Jones, Philip Burne-Jones, Burne-Jones's father, Jenny Morris, Margaret Burne-Jones, Edward Burne-Jones, Jane Morris, William Morris, and May Morris.*

One should be careful not to interpret Morris's poetry in too strict an autobiographical sense, but it is likely, nonetheless, that Morris's reserved nature found some relief in self-expression through it. This is surely the case with the poems in A *Book of Verse*, a manuscript which Morris illuminated and gave to Georgiana Burne-Jones for her 30th birthday in 1870. He derived great comfort and support from his friendship with her, feeling an affection which, had it not been for her rectitude, might have developed into romantic love. As it was she became a very close friend on whose loving sympathy he could rely. He was able to feel particularly at ease with her, knowing that she was in a similar situation; Burne-Jones had fallen in love with a beautiful Greek woman, Mary Zambaco, planning at one point to elope with her. Also a source of support to Morris was his friendship with Mrs

Aglaia Coronio, daughter of Constantine Ionides, a wealthy Greek merchant and patron of the arts; in spite of her affection for him, relationship never developed beyond this. In his correspondence with her he did not conceal his unhappiness, or his struggle for equanimity. In 1872 he wrote:

> *One thing wanting ought not to go for so much: nor indeed does it spoil my enjoyment of life always, as I have often told you: to have real friends and some sort of aim in life is so much, that I ought still to think myself lucky: and often in my better moods I wonder what it is in me that throws me into such rage and despair at other times.*

Morris also found compensation for his unhappy personal life in work, in particular in a new interest. The chivalric ideals, especially that of romantic love, which he had absorbed from medieval literature, no longer seemed a

sufficient guide to life. Something tougher and sterner was needed, and Morris found this in the Icelandic sagas. He began translating them in 1868 with Eirikr Magnusson, an Icelander who was both Morris's tutor and his collaborator. With characteristic impatience he learnt the vocabulary and grammar as he went along, and the first translation, of *The Saga of Gunnlaug*, completed in two weeks, was published in January 1869. It was followed by

*The Grettis Saga* in the same year and *The Volsunga Saga* in 1870. Encouraged by Magnusson, he began to rework some of the stories of the sagas in his own poetry; one of the stories in *The Earthly Paradise*, 'The Lovers of Gudrun', was taken from *The Laxdaela Saga*. The sagas inspired Morris to write what is now often considered his finest piece of poetry, *Sigurd the Volsung*, published in 1876. To Georgiana he listed some of the qualities which he loved in the Norse sagas: '. . . all men's children in it [The Volsunga Saga] . . . so venerable to each other, and so venerated: and the exceeding good temper of Gunnar amidst his heroism, and the calm of Njal . . . what a glorious outcome of the worship of Courage these stories are'. The absolute unyielding stoicism of these characters in adversity was what Morris sought with some success to emulate during the emotional storms of the late 1860s and early 1870s.

In 1871 a resolution of sorts was reached with the leasing of Kelmscott Manor. Leaving Jane and Rossetti to spend the summer there, Morris departed on 6 July for the first trip to Iceland. He was accompanied by Magnusson, Faulkner and a recent acquaintance, Mr WH Evans. He returned at the end of August. This trip inspired and revitalized him. Iceland was little visited at this time and was still fairly primitive. Mackail records that 'the journey was . . . one that had to be taken in adventurous explorers' fashion, with guides and a string of packhorses, carrying tents and food and all means of life: once inland, the traveller was beyond all reach of news: it was a prolonged picnic spiced by hard living and rough riding'.

The beauty and power of the bleak volcanic landscape made a lasting impression on Morris. Most of all, however, he admired the people and the uncomplaining courage with which they led a life of great physical hardship. Moreover, he saw here for the first time a pre-industrial society in which people were united,

LEFT *Kelmscott Manor, the Elizabethan manor-house near the banks of the Thames in Gloucestershire, which Morris took on a joint lease with Rossetti in 1871. This country retreat was to be a great solace to him in later years.*

RIGHT *Iceland in 1890s, Royal Geographic Society. Morris was inspired and revitalized by his trips to Iceland in 1871 and 1873. He particularly admired the courage and comradeship of the people.*

not divided, by hardship; later, when he had become a socialist, he wrote, 'I learnt one lesson there, thoroughly I hope, that the most grinding poverty is a trifling evil compared with the inequality of classes'. A second visit in 1873 reinforced the impression the country had made on him. He wrote to Aglaia Coronio on his return:

> . . . the glorious simplicity of the terrible & tragic, but beautiful land with its well remembered stories of brave men, killed all querulous feeling in me, and have made all the dear faces of wife & children, and love, & friends dearer than ever to me . . . surely I have gained a great deal and it was no idle whim that drew me there, but a true instinct for what I needed.

Another great consolation in Morris's life was his love of Kelmscott Manor. He discovered the house in the spring of 1871. An Elizabethan manor house with 17th-century additions, it was built of local stone and situated close to

the banks of the Thames in the little village of Kelmscott, near Lechlade, in Gloucestershire. Until the joint tenancy with Rossetti ended in 1874, Morris did not spend much time there; Rossetti's obsession with Jane and his irregular habits made his company increasingly antipathetic to Morris. He complained to Aglaia Coronio in 1872:

> . . . another quite selfish business is Rossetti has set himself down at Kelmscott as if he never meant to go away; and not only does that keep me away from that harbour of refuge (because it is really a farce our meeting when we can help it) but also he has all sorts of ways so unsympathetic with the sweet simple old place, that I feel his presence there a kind of slur on it.

In fact Rossetti's health was now breaking down; he was suffering from paranoia and in 1872 attempted suicide by taking an overdose of laudanum (as his wife had done 10 years earlier). He was never entirely to regain mental

LEFT *The drawing room, Kelmscott Manor. The armchairs are covered with 'Peacock and Dragon', a woven woollen fabric, designed by Morris. The walls and curtains were white in Morris's day and reflect his taste for simple, uncluttered interiors. On the right is a drawing of Jane Morris by Rossetti.*

stability; in 1874, partly because of the effect she feared Rossetti might have on her children, Jane ended the affair. She remained on affectionate terms with Rossetti and corresponded with him until his early death in 1882 at the age of 53. From then on Kelmscott Manor became an increasingly precious refuge from the dirt and fatigue of London; Morris had always regarded living in London as a necessity, not a pleasure. He was a keen fisherman and a lover of the countryside. Morris's feelings for Kelmscott Manor and for the natural world are expressed in his utopian novel, *News from Nowhere* (1890), where the house forms the setting for the final scene. Here the feelings expressed by Ellen, the girl with whom the narrator falls in love, are very much those of Morris; 'She led me up close to the house, and laid her shapely sun browned hand and arm on the lichened wall as if to embrace it, and cried out, "O me! O me! How I love the earth, and the seasons, and weather, and all things

that deal with it, and that grows out of it – as this has done!".' In 1882 he wrote of Kelmscott Manor, 'it has come to be to me the type of the pleasant places of the earth, and of the homes of harmless simple people not over-burdened with the intricacies of life; and as others love the race of men through their lovers or their children, so I love the earth through that small space of it'.

In 1875 Morris's business partnership with Rossetti ended when the Firm was reconstituted. It was years since any of the original members of the Firm, except Morris, had played any part in its administration. It was reasonable that the company should now be dissolved and reformed in a way which more closely corresponded to its day-to-day running. In spite of the personal rift between Rossetti and Morris, this was achieved without bad feeling, except on the part of Ford Madox Brown, and the Firm was hence forward known simply as Morris and Company.

RIGHT 'Larkspur'
wallpaper, 1872, an
early Morris design.
From 1875 this
design was also used
for textiles.

The visits to Iceland gave Morris new life, and in the early 1870s he threw himself into his work as a designer. He started designing wallpapers again in 1871, beginning with a series of geometrical patterns, 'Diapers', 'Indian' and 'Venetian'. In 1872, with the intricate but naturalistic 'Jasmine', Morris began his best work in wallpaper design. He produced 17 fine patterns in four years, including 'Vine', 'Willow', 'Apple', 'Larkspur' and 'Marigold'. As with his earliest designs, he turned to English gardens and orchards for inspiration, as he said in a lecture at the Working Men's College in 1881: 'I, as a Western man and a picture lover, must still insist in plenty of meaning to your patterns. I must have unmistakable suggestions of gardens and fields and strange trees, boughs and tendrils ...'. After the very earliest designs there is rarely any degree of abstraction. These designs demonstrate to the full Morris's superb sense of form and colour. They are full of life, yet never tire the eye.

During the 1860s the Firm's output had been mainly ecclesiastical; now its domestic work began to increase and Morris began designing more for the domestic market. In 1873 he designed his first chintz, 'Tulip and Willow', and had it printed by a leading calico-printer, Thomas Clark of Preston. However, he thought the quality of the colour so poor that he was unwilling to sell it. In the first half of the 19th century vegetable dyes had been superseded by new chemical, or aniline, dyes, whose effects were sometimes crude and harsh. Morris objected to the new dyes on technical as well as aesthetic grounds; their colours were often fugitive, that is, liable to fade quickly, and prone to bleeding. 'Tulip and Willow' had been printed in Prussian blue instead of indigo, and the unsatisfactory result spurred Morris to experiment with dyeing techniques.

In 1872 Morris was able to move his family

LEFT Morris dressed in hat and smock for work in the dye-house. In 1875 Morris, in collaboration with Thomas Wardle, began experiments with vegetable dyes.

out of Queen Square to Horrington House in Turnham Green, thus creating room for a small dye-house on the Firm's premises. However, not a great deal could be done on this scale and Morris's period of intense experimentation did not really begin until 1875, when he was able to collaborate with Thomas Wardle, who had a dye-works at Leek in Staffordshire. For Morris, quality in the decorative arts was all important and he preferred not to do something rather than to do it badly; he told Wardle in 1875, 'I am ... as you must know most deeply impressed with the importance of our having all our dyes the soundest & best that can be, and am prepared to give up all that part of my business which depends on textiles if I fail in getting them so'. He visited Leek frequently, and, dressed in sabots and blouse, worked in the dye-house; he enjoyed the business of dyeing, which involved physical hard work and great skill.

RIGHT 'Snakeshead' printed cotton, 1876, designed by Morris; one of his own favourites.

Already the old techniques had almost been forgotten, and Morris and Wardle often had difficulty knowing where to begin. Morris learnt what he could from a wide range of sources, in particular 16th- and 17th-century herbals and manuals on dyeing, often in French and Italian, and from attempts to get the right colours by boiling up twigs. The two men exchanged ideas and Wardle kept Morris informed of progress through a lengthy correspondence. Indigo-dyeing, which Morris was most anxious to perfect, was a particular challenge; it was a delicate and difficult process, but very rewarding when it was successful. The indigo oxidizes and becomes insoluble on contact with the air, as Morris describes in this letter of 1876 to Aglaia Coronio:

> . . . this morning I assisted at the dyeing of 20 lbs. of silk (for our damask) in the blue vat; it was very exciting, as the thing is quite unused now, and we ran a good chance of spoiling the silk. There were four dyers and Mr. Wardle at work, and myself as dyers' mate: the men were encouraged with beer and to it they went, and pretty it was to see the silk coming green coming out of the vat and gradually turning blue . . .

Some of the first designs to be printed by Wardle, for instance, 'Larkspur' and 'Marigold', had already been used for wallpapers. But many new ones were produced; in 1878 Wardle was printing 14, including more flower-based designs, such as 'Honeysuckle', 'Bluebell', 'Iris' and 'Peony', the latter designed by Kate Faulkner. In her book on Morris textiles, Linda Parry points out that some of these early designs, in particular 'Indian Diaper', 'Snakeshead' – Morris's favourite design from this period – 'Little Chintz' and 'Pomegranate', show that Morris was influenced by contemporary Indian textiles. By 1878 Morris had really achieved as much as he could without opening his own factory, but the situation was not completely satisfactory, as he could not exercise sufficient control over the work in Staffordshire to ensure consistent results.

Some idea of Morris's phenomenal energy is gained when one realizes that during the time that he was busy experimenting with dyeing he also wrote a translation of the Aeneid (1875), and in 1876 published Sigurd the Volsung.

LEFT 'Marigold' printed cotton, by Morris, first used as a wallpaper, registered as a textile design in 1875.

RIGHT *Punch cartoon, 15 July, 1876, satirizing Disraeli's indifference to the Turkish massacre of Bulgarian men, women, and children. Morris's outrage at Disraeli's support of the Turks in their war with Russia prompted his first active involvement in politics. He became treasurer of the Eastern Question Association.*

THE SPHINX IS SILENT.

LEFT *Linoleum designed by Morris in 1875, available in two colourways. This was Morris's only design for this medium, although linoleum was very popular at this time.*

Nor were these years free from further personal difficulties and sorrows; in 1876 the health of Morris's 15-year-old daughter, Jenny, broke down and she was diagnosed as having epilepsy. Before the use of anti-convulsive drugs, this was an extremely serious condition, which could result in severe brain damage, and required constant attendance upon the sufferer. The condition was inherited from Morris's side of the family. According to Bernard Shaw, Morris's awareness of this was the greatest sorrow in his life and he describes how the usually suppressed tenderness of Morris's nature was given full expression in his treatment of his daughter: 'Morris adored Jenny. He could not sit in the same room without his arm round her waist. His voice changed when he spoke to her as it changed to no one else'.

In the late 1870s Morris grew increasingly involved in public affairs. As a young man he had not been unaware of social problems but had felt impotent to bring about any real change, as he explained in a letter of 1856: 'I can't enter into politico-social subjects with any interest, for on the whole I see that things are in a muddle, and I have no power or vocation to set them right in ever so little a degree. My work is the embodiment of dreams in one form or another ...'. Morris continued to be politically passive until finally stirred to outrage by the so-called Eastern Question in 1876. In that year the Turks massacred about 12,000 Christian men, women and children in putting down a revolt by their Bulgarian subjects; subsequent declarations by Disraeli, then Conservative Prime Minister, of support for the Turks in a war against Russia were met by a public outcry. Disraeli was motivated by fear of Russia's expansionist policy and by trade considerations. Gladstone, who had resigned as leader of the Liberal party after his defeat in the General Election of 1874, seized this opportunity to act as the figurehead of a popular movement and in September 1876 published a rousing pamphlet, *The Bulgarian Atrocities and the Question of the East*, of which 200,000 copies were sold within a month.

In October 1876 Morris made his first excursion into public life when his letter, fiercely opposing war with Russia, was published in *The Times*. When later that year the Eastern

RIGHT *Detail from*
The Last
Judgement, *stained
glass by Burne-Jones,*
1876, St Michael and
St Mary Magdalene,
Easthampstead,
Berkshire.

LEFT *Detail from* The Last Judgement, *stained glass by Burne-Jones, 1876, St Michael and St Mary Magdalene, Easthampstead, Berkshire.*

Question Association was formed to organize opposition to war, Morris became treasurer. War broke out between Russia and Turkey in April 1877. The following month Morris's pamphlet, *Unjust War: To the Working Men of England*, was published. It contained a bitter attack on those who were calling for war with Russia:

> *Who are they that are leading us into war? Greedy gamblers on the Stock Exchange, idle officers of the army and navy (poor fellows!), worn out mockers of the clubs, desperate purveyors of exciting war news for the comfortable breakfast tables of those who have nothing to lose by war; and, lastly, in the place of honour, the Tory Rump, that we fools, weary of peace, reason and justice, chose at the last election to represent us. . . .*
> *Working men of England, one word of warning yet: I doubt if you know the bitterness of hatred against freedom and progress that lies at the hearts of a certain part of the richer classes in this country . . . These men cannot speak of your order, of its aims, of its leaders, without a sneer or an insult . . . if you long to lessen these inequalities which have been our stumbling-block since the beginning of the world, then cast aside sloth and cry out against an Unjust War, and urge us of the middle classes to do no less. . . .*

The strength of anti-Russian feeling in the country frightened off Gladstone and the parliamentary Liberals; without their full support the Eastern Question Association collapsed in February 1878. Disraeli managed to gain his ends without resorting to war. Morris's involvement in the Eastern Question Association influenced his future political thinking in two ways. He found himself politically very much in sympathy with the working-class men who had supported the Association, but was disillusioned with parliamentary Liberalism. Finally he was to break with the Liberals altogether when they failed to maintain their anti-imperialist position after gaining office in the General Election of 1880.

In 1877 Morris was instrumental in the founding of the Society for the Protection of Ancient Buildings (SPAB). For some time he had been concerned about the work of architects like Sir George Gilbert Scott, who claimed to be carrying out restoration work on old buildings; this consisted of pulling down later additions and rebuilding them in the original style. Like Ruskin before him, Morris felt that it was impossible to accurately copy work of the distant past and that, in any case, a building which had developed over many centuries had a value of its own which should be respected. The announcement that Scott was about to begin this kind of work on Tewkesbury Abbey was the occasion of the founding of the SPAB; Morris wrote to *The Athenaeum*, suggesting that a society to prevent this kind of vandalism was needed. A meeting was held at the Morris and Company showrooms at which the Society for the Protection of Ancient Buildings was formed, with Morris as its first Secretary.

The SPAB, still active today, was the forerunner of the many conservation groups which now exist. Within five years 'Anti-Scrape', as it was affectionately known, was dealing with over a hundred cases a year. Lethaby records how 'Morris, in the early years, visited buildings for the Society – which perhaps was hardly tactful! At one cathedral, on having some commercial work of stalls shown to him, in pride he burst out: "Why, I could carve them better with my teeth".' A significant amount of the Firm's work had consisted of producing new stained glass for old churches; after the formation of the SPAB, Morris refused further commissions of this kind. With Philip Webb as his faithful companion and co-worker, he visited buildings, served on committees and lectured on behalf of the Society. With restoration going on at a rate of 2,500 churches between 1877 and 1885, the Society's work must often have seemed thankless and Lethaby records Morris as saying, 'It looks as if they will see what we mean just as the last old building is destroyed'.

LEFT *Detail from the south window in the transept, designed by Burne-Jones, made by Morris, Marshall, Faulkner & Co., Jesus College Chapel, Cambridge, 1873.*

# CHAPTER FOUR

# REASONABLE
# LABOUR

'Eyebright' printed
cotton, indigo
discharged, designed
by Morris in 1883.

RIGHT *Kelmscott House, Upper Mall, Hammersmith. Morris lived here from 1878 until his death in 1896. He 'liked to think that the water which ran under his windows at Hammersmith had passed the meadows and grey gables of Kelmscott'. The William Morris Society now has its headquarters in the basement.*

IN MARCH 1878 MORRIS was house-hunting; Horrington House was too small for the needs of his family. His daughters, Jenny and May, were now young ladies of 17 and 16. He sent a favourable report of The Retreat, 26 Upper Mall, to Jane, who was wintering in Italy: ... the house could easily be done up at a cost of money, & might be made very beautiful with a touch of my art ... the situation is certainly the prettiest in London'. Although they both felt that the house was rather a long way from the centre of London, Morris pointed out to Jane that it was probably the best they could afford: 'I don't think you or I could stand a quite modern house in a street, say at Notting Hill: I don't fancy going back among the bugs of 'Bloomsbury ... we might as well live at York as at Hampstead for all we should ever see of our friends'. At least the house was reasonably close to the Burne-Joneses, who were now living at The Grange, North End Lane, Fulham.

On 2 April Morris was able to tell Jane that he had taken it; he wrote optimistically about their future there: 'I do think that people will come and see us at the Retreat (fy on the name!) if only for the sake of the garden & river: we will lay ourselves for company than heretofore ... so let us hope that we shall all grow younger there, my dear'. Certainly for Morris, 44 years old now, the following years were ones of tremendous change and activity and of relative stability in his marriage.

In spite of Morris's dislike of Georgian architecture, over the years Kelmscott House became a much-loved family home. He changed the name from The Retreat, which he thought sounded like a lunatic asylum, to Kelmscott House (after Kelmscott Manor). Mackail records how he 'liked to think that the water which ran under his windows at Hammersmith had passed the meadows and grey gables of Kelmscott'. He spent two happy holidays in 1880 and 1881, rowing up the river from London to Kelmscott with family 'and friends. Kelmscott House, built in the 1790s, is a Georgian building with three storeys, an attic and a basement. Its history is a distinguished one: in 1816 Sir Francis Ronalds constructed the first electric telegraph with eight miles of cable in the garden, and Morris's immediate predecessor, the writer George MacDonald, wrote two of his most popular children's books there, *At the Back of the North Wind* and *The Princess and the Goblin*.

Part of Kelmscott House's charm lies in its position on the edge of the river. May Morris's evocative description of it illuminates Morris's principles of interior decoration, particularly his love of the simple and unpretentious:

> *My father's own rooms, sleeping-room and study, were almost frugally bare; in the study no carpet and no curtains; his writing-table in earlier times a plain deal board and trestles, the walls nearly lined with books; just a fine inlaid Italian cabinet in one corner of the study . . .*
> *Above Father's rooms was the long drawing-room, which he turned into a haven of peace and sweet colour, breathing harmony and simplicity. . . . At the fire-side end of the room stood the Red House painted cabinet . . . on the open hearth was the massive pillared grate Mr Webb had designed for Queen's Square; and at right angles to the hearth the Red House settle caught the gleams of the fire on its tawny yellow panels in winter evenings, and in summer the dancing reflections of the river, while lustre plates above the chimney-piece suggested flushed sunsets and dim moonlight nights beyond the elms. At the other end of the room one saw the discreet glimmer of old glass in closed cupboards sunk in the walls, and on a long narrow table lay a few pots and plates from the Far East. No pictures of course . . . no occasional tables, no chairs like feather-beds, no litter of any sort. Plenty of 'quarter-deck' in which to march up and down when discussions got animated and ideas needed exercise . . . Without, the waving trees, the shining river with splendid sweep and stretch of sun-lit land, and the blue distance of Richmond and the Surrey hills.*

LEFT *'Dove and Rose' woven silk and wool double cloth, designed by Morris, 1879.*

George Bernard Shaw describes how in one room 'there was an oriental carpet so lovely that it would have been a sin to walk on it; consequently it was not on the floor but on the wall and half way across the ceiling', and adds that 'on the supper table there was no table cloth: a thing common enough now among people who see that a table should be itself an ornament and not a clothes horse, but then an innovation so staggering that it cost years of domestic conflict to introduce it'.

The move to Kelmscott House gave Morris opportunities to develop important new aspects of his work as a designer, namely, weaving and designing carpets and tapestries. By the mid-1870s Morris was sufficiently satisfied with the results of his experiments in dyeing to turn his attention to weaving. At first his designs for woven cloth were produced outside the Firm; for instance, 'Honeycomb' and 'Anemone', two early designs, were woven by

RIGHT *The drawing room at Kelmscott House as it was in Morris's day. The 'Bird' hangings were especially designed for the room; on the floor is the Firm's machine-woven 'Lily' carpet; the furniture includes the 'Chaucer' wardrobe and a settle, both designed by Webb.*

HM McCrea in 1876. Most commercial yarns were of course chemically dyed and were not considered by Morris to be good enough; he therefore began supplying yarn dyed by Thomas Wardle to the firms contracted to carry out weaving for the Firm. Clearly it was desirable that Morris should control the whole production process and begin weaving himself. A French weaver named Bazin and his loom were brought over from Lyon and established in Queen Square in the summer of 1877; more space had been made there by the transference of the Firm's showrooms to Oxford Street, and by the earlier removal of Morris and his family to Turnham Green in 1872. After some initial difficulties were solved by employing an old Spitalfields weaver as Bazin's assistant, Morris began to design specifically for his own loom. His first wallpaper, 'Trellis', had combined flowers and birds, the latter drawn by Webb. After making a study of

birds himself, Morris now produced a series of fine patterns incorporating them: 'Bird', which was designed for the drawing room at Kelmscott House, 'Bird and Vine', 'Dove and Rose' and 'Peacock and Dragon'. Inspiration for Morris's woven textiles came from both medieval and Eastern sources.

This success in weaving textiles gave Morris the confidence to begin experiments in the far more ambitious sphere of tapestry-weaving and, further, to undertake the revival of the medieval technique of high-warp tapestry-weaving. Morris considered tapestry to be 'the noblest of the arts of weaving' and felt that it demanded a very high level of design. Mackail records that one of Morris's first actions on moving into Kelmscott House was to have a tapestry loom built in his bedroom, on which he completed his first tapestry, 'Acanthus and Vine'; Morris called this 'Cabbage and Vine' because of his difficulty with the acanthus

LEFT 'Bird' woven wool
double cloth, designed
by Morris in 1878 for
the drawing room at
Kelmscott House.

RIGHT 'Lily' Wilton
pile carpet, designed
by Morris about
1875, machine-woven
by Wilton. One of the
most popular of
Morris's designs for
machine-made
carpets.

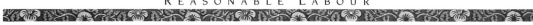

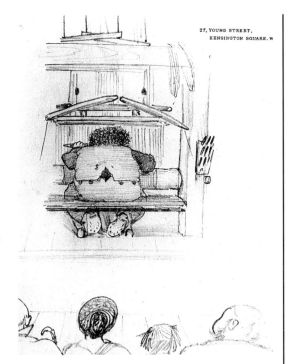

27, YOUNG STREET,
KENSINGTON SQUARE. W

RIGHT *Caricature by Burne-Jones of Morris giving a demonstration of weaving.*

LEFT *'Peacock and Dragon', woven wool, designed by Morris in 1878.*

leaves. It took him 516 hours over a period of four months and was the only tapestry he completely wove himself. He next set up a loom in Queen Square. John Henry Dearle, a young man who was already working in the Firm's glass-painter's shop, was his first assistant and later one of his designers; during his lifetime Burne-Jones was always the Firm's principal designer. It was not until the Firm moved to larger premises at Merton Abbey in 1881 that tapestry-weaving could be undertaken on a commercial scale.

Soon after the move to Kelmscott House, Morris set up carpet looms in the adjoining coach house and stable loft. As with so much of his work as a designer, he began carpet-making because it was difficult to get exactly what he wanted produced outside the Firm. As with Morris's designs for woven textiles, his first carpet designs, which date from about 1873, were contracted out to Heckmondwike Manufacturing Company in Yorkshire and to the Wilton Royal Carpet Works in Wiltshire;

they were machine-made. Just as with the woven textiles produced outside the Firm, Morris was unhappy with the colour of the yarn and again supplied the manufacturer with yarn dyed by Wardle. The inspiration for these early machine-made carpets was again drawn from the flora of the English garden and countryside: 'Rose', 'Wreath', 'Vine', 'Bellflowers' and 'Grass', or 'Daisy'. 'Lily', designed about 1875, was a particularly successful and popular early Wilton carpet. Morris was not, however, entirely happy with these carpets, feeling, as he wrote in the *Arts and Crafts Exhibition Society Catalogue* of 1888, that 'the mechanically-made carpets of today must be looked upon as makeshifts for cheapness sake'. As always, hand-crafting was to be preferred wherever feasible.

Morris was driven to produce his own carpets by a desire to emulate the excellence of Persian carpet-making. He wrote to Wardle in 1877, 'I saw yesterday a piece of *ancient* Persian time of Shah Abbas (our Elizabeth's time) that fairly threw me on my back: I had no

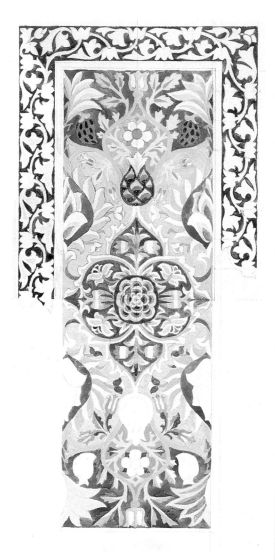

RIGHT *Design for a rug. Morris would draw his carpet designs about one-eighth of the full size, and the drawing would then be transferred to point paper.*

can be identified by the device of a hammer, the letter M and a wavy line, representing the Thames, on their border.

The Firm's expansion into carpet-making and tapestry-weaving, as well as dyeing and cotton-printing, made it essential to find larger workshops. Morris considered moving to the Cotswolds and also back to Kent, but eventually, in 1881, settled on an old print works at Merton Abbey, on the bank of the River Wandle, near Morden in Surrey. The river water was tested for use in madder-dyeing, a process for producing red, and found to be ideal. With a sensitivity which was typical of Morris (although not of the times), he refused to pull down the charmingly picturesque buildings. Instead they were converted into a printing shop, a glass-studio, a weaving factory, and a dye-house; pits for indigo vats were dug; carpet looms were built. The Merton Abbey factory, as Mackail describes it, was idyllic:

> *The works stood on about seven acres of ground, including a large meadow as well as an orchard and vegetable garden . . . . The riverside and the mill pond are thickly set with willows and large poplars; behind the dwelling-house a flower garden, then neglected, but soon restored to beauty when it came into Morris's hands, runs down to the water . . . the cottons lie bleaching on grass thickly set with buttercups; the low long buildings with the clear rushing little stream running between them, and the wooden outside staircases leading to their upper story, have nothing about them to suggest the modern factory; even upon the great sunk dye-vats the sun flickers through leaves, and trout leap outside the windows of the long cheerful room where the carpet-looms are built.*

Merton Abbey's only drawback was the difficulty of access to and from London; Morris furnished a couple of rooms there and often stayed several nights a week. By Christmas 1881 the move from Queen Square to Merton Abbey was complete. The charm of these new surroundings, away from the grime of London,

idea that such wonders could be done in carpets'. From then on more formal and abstract qualities, derived from Eastern art, began to supersede the relative naturalism of Morris's early flower and plant designs. With the assistance of a Glasgow hand-weaver, Morris taught himself the technique of hand-knotting carpets on a carpet frame installed at Queen Square in 1878. Manufacture began properly after the move to Kelmscott House. Girls were trained as carpet-knotters and worked on the premises. Rugs and carpets made at Hammersmith

LEFT 'Flowerpot'
printed cotton, indigo
discharged, designed
by Morris and
registered in 1883.

RIGHT 'Evenlode'
printed cotton, indigo
discharged, designed
by Morris and
registered in 1883,
the first of the Morris
designs to be named
after a tributary of the
Thames.

LEFT *Painting of the pond at Merton Abbey by Lexdon Lewis Peacock (1850–1919). The Firm moved to this idyllic setting on the banks of the River Wandle in Surrey in 1881.*

as well as the possibilities created by the new workshops, stimulated Morris to fresh efforts; the next few years were extremely prolific in terms of design. A new series of chintzes, ie, printed cottons, was produced: between 1881 and 1883 Morris registered at the Patent Office 19 new designs, including what is probably now his best known, 'Strawberry Thief'. Of these, 17 were designed for the indigo discharge technique which Morris was very proud of having developed with Wardle at his dyeworks in Leek. Again floral motifs predominate, with wide differences in scale, ranging from the small-scale, tightly controlled 'Borage', 'Eyebright' and 'Flowerpot', to the large-scale, meandering designs such as 'Evenlode', 'Wey' and 'Windrush'. The delightful 'Brer Rabbit', or 'Brother Rabbit', design, which refers to the Uncle Remus stories of which Morris and his children were fond, dates from these years. Several were named after rivers, including 'Evenlode', named after a tributary of the

Thames, and 'Wandle', named after the river which supplied the water for dyeing at Merton Abbey.

At the same time Morris was designing carpets and tapestries on a scale which was only made possible by the move to Merton Abbey. A loom was installed which could produce a carpet 25 ft (7.5m) wide. Until 1889 the design of the Firm's carpets was almost completely the work of Morris. According to Mackail, he would make a drawing about one-eighth of the full size. This would then be transferred to point paper, that is, squared paper on which each small square represents a single knot of the carpet. Although laborious, this was skilled work and was done by Morris himself until he could train workmen to do it. The same process had to be used for tapestry-weaving. Morris also did a great deal of hand-knotting himself, although generally this work was done by girls, whose smaller hands were nimbler. A visitor to the carpet-weaving factory

RIGHT 'Wey' printed cotton, indigo discharged, designed by Morris about 1883.

LEFT 'Medway' printed cotton, indigo discharged, designed by Morris and registered 1885.

in 1883 described the scene:

> . . . the strong, level afternoon light shines round the figures of the young girls seated in rows on low benches along the frames, and brightens to gold some of the fair heads. Above and behind them rows of bobbins of many-coloured worsteds, stuck on pegs, shower down threads of beautiful colours, which are caught by the deft fingers, passed through strong threads (fixed uprightly in frames, to serve as a foundation) tied in a knot, slipped down in their place, snipped even with the rest of the carpet, all in a second of time.

The carpets which were hand made at Merton Abbey continued to be known as 'Hammersmith rugs', to distinguish them from the machine-made carpets which the Firm was still selling. Knotting carpets by hand was a very labour-intensive activity – a girl could do only 2 in (5cm) of carpet a day – and the carpets were consequently very expensive; the large ones were produced only by commission.

Not surprisingly, the demand for Morris's carpets came principally from the aristocracy and the wealthy middle class, particularly industrialists and entrepreneurs who were using their new wealth to build and decorate country houses and thus establish themselves socially. In 1887 Morris designed a huge carpet, 39 ft (11.7m) long and 12 ft 3 in (3.7m) wide, for Clouds, the Wiltshire home of the Hon Percy Wyndham, designed for him by Philip Webb. The Howards, an aristocratic family, had been clients of Morris since the 1870s and in 1881 he designed a carpet, which took almost a year to complete, for their library at Naworth Castle, ancestral home of the Earls of Carlisle. It was so large that it was not until it was finished that Morris was able to see it whole; he wrote to Howard to explain that the carpet had been finished for a week or two, but that he was waiting for a fine day so he could spread it out on the lawn to see what it looked like. One of Morris's most successful carpets was 'The Bullerswood', made in 1889 for the house of the same name, owned by the Sanderson family. Morris's assistant, JH Dearle, played a part in designing this carpet, which, according to Linda Parry, was the last that Morris designed.

LEFT 'Brer Rabbit'
printed cotton,
designed by Morris,
and registered 1882.
The name of this
design refers to the
Uncle Remus stories
which Morris and his
children enjoyed.

RIGHT 'Holland Park' design Hammersmith carpet. This design was first produced for the home of AA Ionides at 1 Little Holland Park in 1883; Morris used it again for this carpet, made about 1886–9 for Clouds, the country house of the Honourable Percy Wyndham.

LEFT *Oak centre table made by Morris and Company, design attributed to Philip Webb and George Jack, a pupil of Webb's, designed for Clouds in the 1880s or early 1890s.*

Morris's tapestries could similarly be afforded only by the very rich. The first figure tapestry to be woven at Merton Abbey was *The Goose Girl* in 1883, its design taken from Walt Crane's book illustration for *Grimm's Fairy Tales*. Morris was not pleased with the result and decided that adapting designs meant for other mediums did not work. From then on Burne-Jones produced the figure designs, and details of foliage, flowers and even costume were supplied by Morris and, as time went on, also by Dearle. Morris himself produced complete designs for only three tapestries, but one of these, *Woodpecker*, is one of the most successful. Two very popular designs were *Flora* and *Pomona*, both with verses by Morris woven into the border; at least 11 versions of the former exist and six of the latter.

It is ironic that the 1880s, when Morris was producing work which could be afforded only by a small, highly privileged group of people, like the Wyndhams and the Howards, were also the years of Morris's greatest activity and commitment as a socialist. Morris was not unaware of this irony: even in the 1870s Morris had been unhappy about the market at which the Firm's goods, because of their great expense, were necessarily aimed. Lethaby recounts an incident which took place while Morris and the Firm were decorating Rounton Grange, near Northallerton, a house designed by Webb for Sir Lowthian Bell, the ironmaster. 'Sir Lowthian Bell told Mr Alfred Powell that

one day he heard Morris talking and walking about in an excited way, and went to inquire if anything was wrong. He turned on me like a mad animal – "It is only that I spend my life in ministering to the swinish luxury of the rich".' Morris also was becoming increasingly aware of the contrast between his own comfortable and fulfilled existence and the degradation of much of the working class. This awareness is described graphically in a passage from a lecture which Morris gave in 1881:

*As I sit at my work at home, which is at Hammersmith, close by the river, I often hear some of that ruffianism go past the window of which a good deal has been said in the papers of late, and has been said before at recurring periods. As I hear the yells and shrieks and all the degradation cast on the glorious tongue of Shakespeare and Milton, as I see the brutal reckless faces and figures go past me, it arouses the recklessness and brutality in me also, and fierce wrath takes possession of me, till I remember, as I hope I mostly do, that it was my good luck only of being born respectable and rich, that has put me on this side of the window among delightful books and lovely works of art, and not on the other side, in the empty street, the drink-steeped liquor shops, the foul and degraded lodgings. I know by my own feelings and desires what these men want, what would have saved them from this lowest depth of savagery: employment which would foster their self-respect and win the praise and sympathy of their fellows, and dwellings which they could come to with pleasure, surroundings which would soothe and elevate them; reasonable labour, reasonable rest. There is only one thing that can give them this – art.*

Morris had begun public speaking on art and architecture after the foundation of the Society for the Protection of Ancient Buildings in 1877 in order to make the Society's ideas better known and to raise money for its work. In these lectures he explored the relationship between art and society and concluded that the degraded state of contemporary art and design was closely associated with the degraded condition of the workman; he felt that change in either could come about only through radical social reform. By 1883 Morris was beginning to think that the only hope for art and for the working classes lay in revolutionary socialism. In 1885 he wrote, 'when art is fairly in the clutch of profit-grinding she dies, and leaves behind her but her phantom of *sham* art as the futile slave of the capitalist . . .. Socialism . . . is the only hope of the arts'.

Looking around him Morris could not have escaped seeing that industrialization and urbanization had led to vice and moral degradation. Philip Henderson, in his biography of Morris, describes how, 'foreign visitors to London at this time . . . Dostoevsky among them, were appalled at the spectacle of the Haymarket at night, where prostitutes gathered in their thousands, where mothers put up their little daughters for sale and children of twelve seized your arm and wanted to follow you'. Accurate statistics relating to poverty are difficult to come by but a survey carried out in London by Charles Booth in the 1880s estimated that nearly 10 per cent of families were living below the subsistence level, and another 20 just at this level. HMI Fitch, writing in 1870 of slums in Leeds and quoted in Geoffrey Best's *Mid-Victorian Britain 1851–1875*, refers to the poorest 'living a life of indigence, squalor and hopelessness, which it is difficult for comfortable people to conceive. It is known that there are hundreds of families, whose average income from all sources does not exceed 1s per head per week'.

In the late 1870s Morris was looking to Gladstone, 'The People's William', and the Liberal party to bring about the social change that would alleviate the condition of the working class, even though his first association with the Liberals as treasurer of the Eastern Question Association had ended in disillusionment early in 1878. He told Jane, 'as to my political career, I think it is at an end for the present; & has ended sufficiently disgustingly . . .. I am out of it now, I mean as to bothering my head about it: I shall give up reading the Papers, and stick to my work'. But as Mackail explains, 'when the crisis in the East was finally past, it left Morris in touch with the Radical leaders of the working class in London' and it was through his sympathy with them that in the autumn of 1878 he was persuaded to become treasurer of the new National Liberal League. This was a pressure group within the Liberal party, formed by radical, working-class members of the disbanded Eastern Question Association. Its first important campaign was to mobilize working-class support in London for the Liberal party in the election of 1880.

Morris's views were strongly anti-imperialist and formed one of the main grounds of his support of Gladstone. He was therefore particularly dismayed by the Liberal Party's foreign Policy after Gladstone came to power. First in 1881 came the Irish Coercion Bill – a virtual repeal of *habeas corpus* in Ireland – which was intended to counter agricultural unrest following the depression of the 1870s, which had led to an unprecedented number of evictions of Irish tenant-farmers. Then in July 1882 Gladstone ordered the bombardment of Alexandria to restore civil order after a national revolt; after that, the British army occupied Egypt. Both these actions were influenced by the need to maintain control over the Suez Canal.

Outraged by these acts of political expediency, Morris despaired of the Liberal Party: 'The action and want of action of the new

RIGHT Acanthus and Vine, *Morris's first tapestry, which he called 'Cabbage and Vine' because of the difficulty which he had with the acanthus leaves. It was woven in about four months in 1879 on the loom which Morris set up in his bedroom at Kelmscott House.*

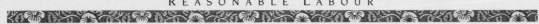

LEFT *Luke Fildes,* Applicants for Admission to a Casual Labour Ward, *oil on canvas, 1874, now at Royal Holloway College, University of London. In the late 1870s Morris was becoming increasingly disturbed by the degradation of the urban poor.*

RIGHT Woodpecker, 1885, one of only three tapestries completely designed by Morris, now in the William Morris Gallery, Walthamstow. The verse is by Morris and was embroidered by May Morris and assistants.

LEFT *Morris and Company embroidered screen, probably designed by May Morris for the drawing room of Bullerswood, the home of the Sanderson family, about 1889.*

Liberal Parliament, especially the Coercion Bill and the Stockjobber's Egyptian war quite destroyed any hope I might have had of any good being done by alliance with the radical party', he wrote to a friend. To Morris's relief the National Liberal League was in any case wound up in November 1882. He had now decided that no really far-reaching reforms would be carried out by a party under middle-class control: 'Radicalism is on the wrong line ... and will never develop into anything more than Radicalism ... it is made for and by the middle classes and will always be under the control of rich capitalists: they will have no objection to its *political* development if they think they can stop it there: but as to real social changes, they will not allow them if they can help it'. On 13 January 1883 he committed himself to socialism by joining the Democratic Federation.

# CHAPTER FIVE

# FELLOWSHIP IS HEAVEN

'Honeysuckle' wallpaper, designed about 1883 probably by May Morris with assistance from Morris. May was a talented designer in her own right as well as an excellent embroideress. She managed the Firm's embroidery section from 1885.

RIGHT *Interior of the*
*Coach House,*
*Kelmscott House, the*
*meeting place of the*
*Hammersmith*
*socialists. Here*
*speakers such as*
*Morris and George*
*Bernard Shaw spoke*
*to audiences of*
*working men and*
*young intellectuals*
*and radicals, such as*
*H. G. Wells and*
*Yeats.*

BECOMING A SOCIALIST at the age of 49 was not a step which Morris took lightly. During the winter of 1882–83 he attended a series of lectures, intended as an introduction to socialism, which were organized by the Democratic Federation. Andreas Scheu, an Austrian refugee who was to be a fellow worker for the socialist cause, remembered seeing Morris, famous at this time as the author of *The Earthly Paradise*, at the first of these meetings:

> . . . *the book-binder, who sat behind me, passed me .*
> *a note . . . 'The third man on your right is William*
> *Morris'. I had never seen Morris before and looked*
> *at once in his direction. The fine, highly intelligent*
> *face of the man, his earnestness, the half-searching,*
> *half-dreamy look of his eyes, his plain*
> *unfashionable dress, made a deep sympathetic*
> *impression on me.*

Although Morris's theoretical knowledge of socialism was at this time very limited, he had read articles arguing the case against socialism by the liberal, John Stuart Mill, and also the work of Henry George, the American sociologist, whose book, *Progress and Poverty*, advocated land nationalization. Immediately after joining the Democratic Federation he read Marx; *Das Kapital* had by this date been translated into French, the language in which Morris read it, but not into English. Although Marx had been living in London since 1849, he died in March 1883 and Morris never met him.

This was a most opportune moment for Morris to become politically involved. Until the early 1880s there had been no organized working-class support of major democratic reform – not since the death of the Chartist movement in the late 1840s. The mid-Victorian period was generally a time of prosperity, rising wages and full employment. The Reform Act of 1867, which extended the franchise to most of the adult male population, was a move towards democratic reform through legislation. It was not until the depressions and unemployment of the 1870s that there was fertile ground for a revival of working-class agitation. At the same time British socialism acquired intellectual new blood from socialist refugees who had fled from persecution on the Continent in the 1870s. The Democratic Federation was formed in 1881 from various Radical clubs; in 1884 it became the Social Democratic Federation and as such was the first British socialist party.

Once convinced of the rightness of socialism, Morris threw himself into the work of the Federation, not allowing himself to be deterred by his dislike and distrust of Henry Mayers Hyndman, the leader of the Democratic Federation and then of the Social Democratic Federation. Hyndman was a former Conservative with a private income who had been converted to socialism by meeting Marx and reading *Das Kapital*. Bernard Shaw was no doubt exaggerating when he claimed that 'of Hyndman's most brilliant conversational performance it was impossible to believe a single word'. Nevertheless, Hyndman was a political opportunist and a manipulator; apart from his fierce temper, which rivalled Morris's, the two men could scarcely have been more different. Morris was willing to tolerate him because of his genuine belief in socialism: he told George Wardle, the business manager of Morris and Company, 'I don't like the man, but as he is trying to do what I think ought to be done, I feel that everyone who has similar ideas ought to help him'.

The Social Democratic Federation aimed to educate the working class and to organize them for the socialist revolution which members of the Federation believed to be imminent. Indeed in his book, *The Historical Basis of Socialism in Britain* (1883), Hyndman had implied that the time would be ripe in 1889, the centenary of the French Revolution. In its staunchly working-class emphasis, the Federation was far more sympathetic to Morris than the Fabian Society, formed in 1884, which consisted mainly of intellectuals and middle-class socialists. Writing in *The Commonweal*, the journal of the Socialist League, in 1890, Morris described the Federation as composed in the early days of 'a few working men, less successful even in the wretched life of labour than their fellows; a sprinkling of the intellectual proletariat ... one or two outsiders in the game political; a few refugees from the bureaucratic tyranny of foreign governments; and here and there an unpractical, half-cracked artist or author'. The oddly assorted comrades included Marx's daughter, Eleanor, and her lover, the scientist Edward Aveling, of whom Shaw, scarcely exaggerating, said, 'he seduced every woman he met and borrowed from every man'. More congenial to Morris was Belfort Bax, a musician and philosopher, with whom he was to collaborate in writing *Socialism, its Growth and Outcome*, published in 1893.

The enrolment of Morris was a coup for the Democratic Federation. He was by far their most eminent member and was able to give considerable financial assistance. Hyndman wrote on Morris's death, 'with his great reputation and high character [he] doubled our strength at a stroke, by giving in his adhesion'. Even before joining the Federation Morris had sold his library to further the socialist cause and, once a member, Hyndman recalls how Morris was:

> ... even too eager to take his full share in the unpleasant part of our public work and speedily showed that he meant to work in grim earnest on the same level as the rank and file of our party .... He was never satisfied unless he was doing things which, to say the truth, he was little fitted for, and others of coarser fibre could do much better than he.

Morris soon became the Democratic Federation's treasurer and largely financed its weekly paper, *Justice*, first published in January 1884, in addition to writing about half its contents. Along with Hyndman and others from the Federation, he also sold it on street corners. He established a branch of the Federation in Hammersmith, with his own workmen as members. There were regular Sunday meetings in the coach house at Kelmscott House; sometimes these took the form of art evenings, a very middle-class form of entertainment. Bernard Shaw and Annie Besant, who led the match-girls' strike in 1888 and was later a well-known feminist and theosophist, sang duets at the piano and Morris and Aveling read poetry. The Hammersmith Social Democratic Federation choir sang especially composed songs from Morris's *Chants for Socialists*. Morris designed the Federation's membership card and, most taxing of all, he undertook an arduous programme of public speaking. Through this he made a profound impression on many members of his audience. A young socialist, Bruce Glasier, who heard him speak in Glasgow and Edinburgh in 1884, remembered those occasions vividly:

*He was then fifty-one years of age, and just beginning to look elderly. His splendid crest of dark curly hair and his finely textured beard were brindling into grey. His head was lion-like – not only because of his shaggy mane, but because of the impress of strength of his whole front . . .. I noted the constant restlessness of his hands, and indeed of his whole body, as if overcharged with energy . . .. He read his lecture, or rather recited it, keeping his eyes on the written pages, which he turned over without concealment . . . every now and then [he] walked to and fro, bearing his manuscript schoolboy-like, in his hand. Occasionally he paused in his recital, and in a 'man to man' sort of way explained some special point, or turned to those near him on the platform for their assent . . .. Of the lecture itself I only remember that it seemed to me something more than a lecture, a kind of parable or prediction, in which art and labour were held forth, not as mere circumstances or incidents to life, but as life or the act of living itself.*

Not only did Morris's devotion to socialism mean a great sacrifice of time and money, it also meant that to a large extent he was estranged from friends and peers. Georgiana Burne-Jones sympathized but her husband, although he felt that Morris was right, did not have the courage to join him: 'it was the only time I failed Morris', Georgiana Burne-Jones recorded him as saying. Their friendship suffered, partly through a lessening of sympathy between them and partly because Morris simply had far less time to give to friends who were not also involved in working for the cause. Of his contemporaries the faithful Webb and Faulkner were the only ones to follow him into the socialist camp. Morris did, however, derive great comfort from the support of his daughters, particularly May. She began accompanying him to meetings of the Social Democratic Federation from its inception in January 1884, and was to play a full and independent part in the work for socialism. Many, however, regarded Morris as a traitor, if not to his country at least to his class, and thought that he was associating with dangerous anarchists and nihilists. His allegiance to the socialist cause was deplored in the press, but he was not deterred.

Morris regarded himself as a communist. His adoption of the socialist cause was at first based on an instinctive response to what he felt to be injustice. In Marx's account of the alienation of the worker in an industrial society, and of his liberation through the class struggle, he found a theoretical base to underpin these instincts. He summed up his position in a letter to CE Maurice in July 1883:

*In looking into matters social and political I have but one rule, that in thinking of the condition of any body of men I should ask myself, 'How could you bear it yourself? What would you feel if you were poor against the system under which you live?' . . . the answer to it has more and more made me ashamed of my own position, and more and more*

LEFT *Membership card of the Democratic Federation designed by Morris. Morris joined the Democratic Federation in 1883; it became the Social Democratic Federation in 1884, and was the first British socialist party.*

*made me feel that if I had not been born rich or well-to-do I should have found my position unendurable, and should have been a mere rebel against what would have seemed to me a system of robbery and injustice. Nothing can argue me out of this feeling, which I say plainly is a matter of religion to me: the contrasts of rich and poor are unendurable and ought not be endured by either rich or poor. Now it seems to me that . . . I am bound to act for the destruction of the system which seems to me mere oppression and obstruction; such a system can only be destroyed, it seems to me, by the united discontent of numbers; isolated acts of a few persons of the middle and upper classes seeming to me . . . quite powerless against it: in other words the antagonism of classes, which the system has bred, is the natural necessary instrument of its destruction. . . . I am quite sure that the change which will overthrow our present system will come sooner or later: on the middle classes to a great extent it depends whether it will come peacefully or violently.*

The contradiction between Morris's socialist views and his position as a wealthy, middle-class businessman was from the first pointed out by his critics. They felt that to be consistent he should distribute the Firm's profits among its workmen. Morris's workmen do not appear to have been disturbed by this inconsistency, perhaps because Morris treated them with respect as fellow workers, and also paid them more than average wages. Some of Morris's justification for not profit-sharing can be gathered from the above-quoted passage; he felt that individual tinkering with the system was useless – it must be overthrown in its entirety. He regarded revolution, whether violent or not, as a historical necessity which would certainly come in his lifetime. Nevertheless, he did feel uneasy about the situation and in 1884 worked out the consequences of taking such a step. According to his calculations each workman would receive an extra £16 a year. As he explained in a letter to Georgiana: 'that I admit [would] be a very nice thing for them, but it would not alter the position of any one of them, but would leave them still members of the working class with all the disadvantages of that position'. Moreover, he was not the only one who would be affected by such a decision:

RIGHT *Photograph of the Hammersmith branch of the Socialist League. Morris is fifth from the right in the second row. May, wearing a light dress, is in the centre of the front row. Jenny is second to the left of her.*

> *. . . there are those other partners called my family: now you know we ought to be able to live upon £4 a week . . . but here comes the rub, and I feel the pinch of society for which society I am only responsible in a very limited degree. And yet if Janey & Jenny were quite well and capable I think they ought not to grumble at living on the said £4, nor do I think they would.*

However, Jenny was an invalid who needed constant care, and Jane, possibly in part because of the strain of looking after her, was also often far from well. In fact Morris did carry out a form of profit-sharing, limited to a few of the most important of his employees, but essentially the Firm remained as it was.

In December 1884 there was a split in the Social Democratic Federation. Ostensibly this was caused by a disagreement about tactics, but a clash of personalities lay beneath it. Hyndman was dictatorial, devious and vain; his genuine belief in socialism coexisted with a desire to use the Federation as a vehicle for his parliamentary ambition. He wanted the Federation to become a conventional political party, campaigning for reforms and, as soon as possible, putting up candidates for local and parliamentary elections. At the SDF conference in June 1884 it was decided not to put up parliamentary candidates and Hyndman was displaced as president; instead members of the executive took turns to act as chairman. This may have accorded more with certain socialist principles but it was emphatically not to Hyndman's taste, as Morris realized, explaining to a colleague at the time of the split, 'Hyndman is determined to be master, and will not accept any other place, and he cannot change his nature and be other than a jingo and a politician even if he tries'.

Morris did not oppose getting members into parliament once the Federation had a strong enough base, but he did not feel that it should be their aim at all costs, as Hyndman did. In particular he was very much opposed to sordid electioneering and to gaining concessions by doing deals with other parties. Along with others in the Federation, he felt that their principal aim should be the preparation of the working classes for their part in the coming revolution: 'Education towards Revolution seems to me to express in three words what our policy should be', Morris later declared. Early on Morris had understood that there were serious divisions within the Federation. He wrote to Georgiana Burne-Jones in August 1883:

> Small as our body is, we are not without dissensions in it. Some of the more ardent member look upon Hyndman as too opportunist, and there is truth in that; he is sanguine of speedy change happening somehow, and is inclined to intrigue and the making of a party. . . . I . . . think the aim of Socialists should be the founding of a religion, towards which end compromise is no use, and we only want to have those with us who will be with us to the end.

After months of Hyndman's intrigue and infighting, and despite Morris's efforts to act as peacemaker, the crisis came in December 1884. Morris resigned, taking with him Eleanor Marx, Aveling and Belfort Bax. With the support of Engels, Marx's closest collaborator, they established an alternative socialist organization, the Socialist League. Morris much regretted the split, realizing that it had seriously weakened the socialist cause, and hoped that before long socialists might be united in one party again. Meanwhile the two associations managed to stay on fairly amicable terms.

Morris's work for the Firm was by now reduced to a minimum, although he still turned out an occasional design when it was needed. Fortunately, the Firm was able to continue running smoothly under the business management of George Wardle, while Dearle was in day-to-day control at Merton Abbey. In 1885,

May took over the management of the embroidery section of the Firm; she was by this time a skilled embroiderer and had also done some designing. For many years Morris had spent Sunday mornings at The Grange with the Burne-Joneses; these visits ceased as over the next five years he threw himself even more completely into working for the cause. The number of committed socialists was at this time extremely small; when Morris resigned, the Social Democratic Federation numbered only about 500. Morris saw his role as essentially one of propagandist, educating the working classes in socialist theory. As he explained in an interview with the Liberal newspaper, Daily News, in January 1885, 'the discontented must know what they are aiming at when they overthrow the old order of things. My belief is that the old order can only be overthrown by force, and for that reason it is all the more important that the revolution . . . should not be an ignorant, but an educated revolution'. By the summer of 1886 the Socialist League had a membership of about 700.

Morris's political work took two forms, writing and public speaking. He was well aware of his deficiencies as a speaker, particularly before a working-class audience; 'it is a great drawback that I can't speak roughly to them and unaffectedly', he told Georgiana, 'you see this great class gulf lies between us'. Writing lectures he regarded as a laborious chore. Nevertheless, he lectured 120 times between 1885 and 1886, touring East Anglia, Yorkshire, Lancashire, Yorkshire and Scotland, even travelling as far as Dublin. In addition he played a full part in the Socialist League's campaign of open-air speaking; the Sunday mornings formerly given over to the Burne-Joneses were devoted to this. Despite the failures of his delivery and his tendency to speak above the heads of his audience, his sincerity was impressive; so was the simple fact that such a famous man was prepared to devote so much time to speaking on street corners or visiting the East End to address sometimes a mere handful of working men.

A severe trade recession in the mid-1880s brought high unemployment and a receptive audience. Attempts by the police to suppress socialist speakers addressing crowds in public places created a good deal of unrest and also a great deal of publicity for socialism. It united disparate radical and socialist groups, including even the Fabians, who favoured a gradualist approach, in opposition to the police. The Socialist League offered support to the Social Democratic Federation after charges of obstruction were brought against its speakers in the summer of 1885. In September Morris himself was arrested and brought before a magistrate, accused of striking a policeman and breaking the strap on his helmet during an uproar in court after a socialist speaker had been sentenced to two month's hard labour, having been found guilty of obstruction. Morris denied the charge, and when questioned about his identity, replied, 'I am an artistic and literary man, pretty well known, I think, throughout Europe'. He was allowed to go free.

Morris's arrest was the best possible publicity for the Socialist League; it was reported as far afield as the United States and rallied supporters to the cause of free speech. The contrast between the court's treatment of Morris and of his working-class comrades was highlighted both on this occasion and in the following August, when Morris and two others, working men named Williams and Mainwaring, were arrested for obstruction. Morris was fined only a shilling because, the judge explained, 'as a gentleman', Morris 'would at once see, when it was pointed out to him, that such meetings were a nuisance, and would desist in taking part in them'. Williams and Mainwaring were fined £20 and bound over to keep the peace for 12 months. Unable to pay, they were

sent to prison for two months. Morris embarrassed the authorities and the police who did not know how to deal with him and were reluctant to arrest him. Well aware of this, Morris tried to be present as often as possible when there was liable to be trouble with the police, who were often brutal in their treatment of working-class agitators.

On 13 November 1887 – 'Bloody Sunday' – a meeting which had first been called to protest against Coercion in Ireland became a huge demonstration in defence of free speech in Trafalgar Square, attracting support from all radical and socialist organizations. Processions attempting to enter the square in defiance of an official ban were broken up by police charges in which two of the demonstrators were killed and 200 treated in hospital. The following Sunday a young workman, Alfred Linnell, died after being ridden down by a mounted policeman in Northumberland Avenue, a road leading out of Trafalgar Square. his death became a focus for popular outrage, and the procession at his funeral on 16 December was the largest in London since the death of Wellington in 1852. Morris was one of the pallbearers and made a moving speech by the graveside. The funeral ended with the crowd singing 'A Death Song', which was composed by Morris for the occasion and sold for Linnell's orphans as a broadsheet designed by Walter Crane.

In addition to this gruelling and sometimes dangerous testimony on behalf of socialism in working men's clubs and on the streets, Morris was also writing extensively for the cause. The first number of The Commonweal, the journal of the Socialist League, was published in February 1885, just a month after the foundation of the League, with Morris as editor and Aveling as sub-editor. At first it was a monthly; it became a weekly, with Morris as sole editor, in May 1886. This meant a tremendous burden of work for Morris, who also financed the paper

LEFT *Photograph of Morris by Hollyer taken in 1886, when Morris was intensely preoccupied with his work for socialism.*

BELOW *'The Attitude of the Police', 1886, a cartoon referring to the deferential attitude of the police towards Morris, who, unlike his working-class colleagues, was allowed to carry out his public speaking on behalf of socialism more or less with impunity.*

THE ATTITUDE OF THE POLICE.
(DEDICATED TO "THE FORCE," MR. SAUNDERS, AND THE SOCIALISTS.)

RIGHT *Frontispiece to the Kelmscott Press edition of Morris's Utopian novel,* News from Nowhere, *first published in serial form in* The Commonweal, *the journal of the Socialist League, in 1890.*

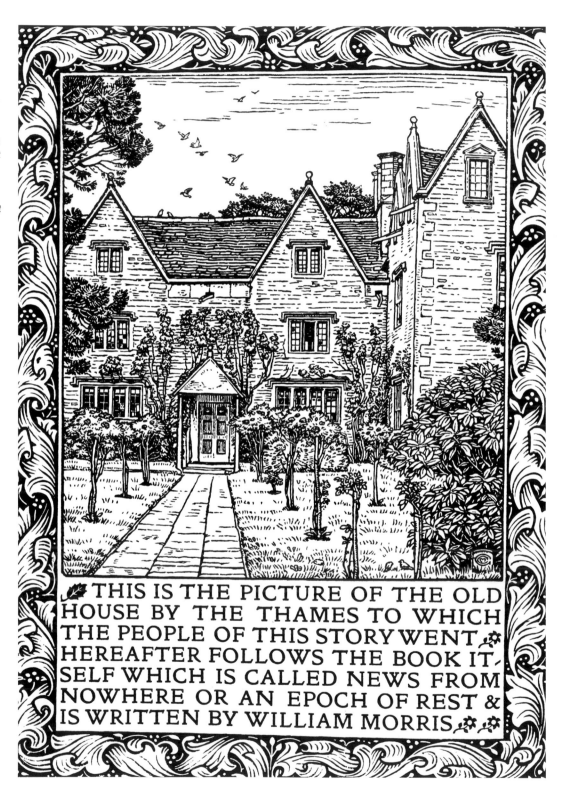

THIS IS THE PICTURE OF THE OLD HOUSE BY THE THAMES TO WHICH THE PEOPLE OF THIS STORY WENT HEREAFTER FOLLOWS THE BOOK IT SELF WHICH IS CALLED NEWS FROM NOWHERE OR AN EPOCH OF REST & IS WRITTEN BY WILLIAM MORRIS

and acted as the League's treasurer. He was also one of the principal contributors to *The Commonweal*, in which two of his major late works, *The Dream of John Ball* and *News from Nowhere*, were published in serial form.

Although most of his writing in the 1880s was related to socialism in one way or another, he also managed to find time to write a verse translation of Homer's *Odyssey*, which was published in 1887. Of interest chiefly because of its autobiographical content is Morris's *The Pilgrims of Hope*, which was published in *The Commonweal* between March 1885 and July 1886. It is set at the time of the Paris Commune in 1870; the hero's loss of his wife to his best friend and his subsequent work as a revolutionary socialist clearly reflect Morris's own experience. Morris often found the round of lectures dreary and thankless, as is made clear by this description of the hero, dressed in the indigo blue suit which Morris had adopted and addressing a radical club:

> Dull and dirty the room . . .
> Some thirty men we were of the type that I knew full well,
> Listless, rubbed down to the type of our easy-going hell.
> . . . He rose, thickset and short, and dressed in shabby blue
> . . . He spoke, were it well, were it ill, as though a message he bore,
> . . . But they sat and made no sign, and two of the glibber kind
> Stood up to jeer and to carp, his fiery words to blind.
> . . . I rose ere the meeting was done
> And gave him my name and my faith – and I was the only one.

Morris often despaired at the apathy of the men he was trying to convert, but he also understood and sympathized with their demoralization: 'If I were to spend ten hours a day at work I despised and hated, I should spend my leisure, I hope, in political agitation, but, I fear, in drinking'.

'Fellowship is heaven, and lack of fellowship is hell'. These words from *A Dream of John Ball* are very much an expression of Morris's own sentiments. They are spoken by John Ball, the leader of the Peasants' Revolt of 1331. *The Dream of John Ball* is a prose romance in which the narrator visits the past in a dream; what he learns of fellowship from John Ball, and the beauty of his vision of the Middle Ages, inspire him when he awakes to a dirty, dreary industrial London.

In *News from Nowhere*, published in serial form in *The Commonweal* between January and October 1890, Morris looked to the future for hope. This utopian novel is perhaps the most accessible of Morris's writings for the modern reader. In it the narrator falls asleep in Hammersmith and wakes up in the future. A socialist revolution has taken place in 1952 and the narrator finds an ideal society in which people work for pleasure, mechanization and private property have been abolished, and there is no money. There is equality of class and sex, and there are no cities; people live in smaller rural communities, working on the land and at hand-crafts in harmony with the natural world.

By the time he wrote *News from Nowhere*, Morris had come to realize that the hoped-for revolution was further away than he had thought. The Socialist League was falling apart. On the one hand Eleanor Marx, Aveling and Bax were feeling, as Hyndman had done, that socialism should engage with the parliamentary system. On the other, the League was being taken over by anarchists, who voted Morris out of the editorship of *The Commonweal* at the 1890 conference. Morris withdrew the Hammersmith branch from the League. It was his money – he had been giving £500 a year to the League – and his energy which had held the League together; it now split up into dissenting factions.

CHAPTER SIX

# OUR BEST MAN

*'Iris' wallpaper,
designed by Dearle.
He became a partner
of the Firm and art
director after Morris's
death in 1896.*

RIGHT The Adoration of the Magi, *tapestry designed by Burne-Jones in 1887 and woven by Morris & Company in 1890. Presented by Morris and Burne-Jones as a gift to Exeter College of which they had been made Honorary Fellows in 1883.*

*The last time I saw Morris [wrote James Leatham, a young member of the Social Democratic Federation] he was speaking from a lorry pitched on a piece of waste land close to the Ship Canal . . .. It was a wild March Sunday morning, and he would not have been asked to speak out of doors, but he had expressed a desire to do so, and so there he was, talking with quiet strenuousness, drawing a laugh now and then from the undulating crowd, of working men mostly, who stood in the hollow and on the slopes before him. There would be quite two thousand of them. He wore a blue overcoat, but had laid aside his hat; and his grizzled hair blew in wisps and tumbles about his face . . .. In spite of the bitter cold of the morning, scarcely a man moved from the crowd; though there was comparatively little fire or fervour in the speech, and next to no allusion to any special topic of the hour. Many there were hearing and seeing the man for the first time; most of us were hearing him for the last time; and we all looked and listened as though we knew it.*

MORRIS WAS SPEAKING for the Social Democratic Federation in Manchester in 1894. The

above account gives some idea of why his health broke down in 1891; the sheer physical strain of speaking outdoors in all weather up and down the country must have been in part to blame. Weariness of spirit after the break-up of the Socialist League in 1890 and constant anxiety over the worsening condition of Morris's epileptic daughter, Jenny, who was gravely ill early in 1891, also played their part. In February 1891 Morris was very ill with gout; according to Mackail 'his kidneys were found to be gravely affected; and he was told that henceforth he must 'consider himself an invalid to the extent of husbanding his strength and living under a very careful regimen'. It is possible that this was the onset of the diabetes from which he died in 1896.

Morris could no longer be prodigal of his energies and a ordering of priorities took place. In a letter of 1892 he told Bruce Glasier, the young Scottish socialist, that 'at present the

absolute *duties* of my life are summed up in the necessity of taking care of my wife and daughter …. My *work* of all kinds is really simply an amusement taken when I can out of my duty time'. He continued to work for socialism, but at the reduced rate which was all his health permitted; he chaired meetings of the Hammersmith Socialist Society, the group which he had established after the break-up of the Socialist League, and continued to speak at outdoor meetings. He still hoped for a united British Socialist Party, and negotiated, unsuccessfully, to bring that about in 1892 to 1893. He was pleased by the election to Parliament in 1892 of the first three Independent Labour Party MPs, regarding 'this obvious move forward of the class-feeling' as '… full of real hope'. To a certain extent he was aloof from the fray in these last years and the fact that he was known to be speaking not for one particular faction, but in the interests

of socialism as a whole, increased his influence.

Nevertheless, the true solace of Morris's last years lay not in politics, but in a new undertaking, the founding of the Kelmscott Press, and in the revival of an interest which went back to his days as an undergraduate, collecting early printed books and 13th-century manuscripts. Morris's earliest inspiration for the Kelmscott Press was a lecture by Emery Walker on printing, which he attended at the Arts and Crafts Exhibition on 15 November 1888. Walker, an extremely knowledgeable amateur printer, was already well known to Morris, for he had been secretary of the Hammersmith branch of the Social Democratic Federation at its foundation in 1884, and also lived near him in Hammersmith. Morris relied very much on his advice in setting up the Kelmscott Press and would have liked him to become a partner. Although Walker declined, he nonetheless played a major part in its

RIGHT *Escritoire and stand designed by George Jack and made by Morris and Company, 1893. Jack, who was trained by Philip Webb, became the Firm's chief furniture designer in 1890. This example with its unoriginal but attractive marquestry decoration is typical of his work.*

LEFT *Morris's bed at Kelmscott Manor with hangings and cover designed by May Morris about 1893. The cover was embroidered by Jane Morris and the hangings were worked by May assisted by Lily Yeats, sister of the poet, and Ellen Wright. The verse is by Morris.*

running. With the thoroughness and determination with which Morris always tackled any skill or craft he had decided to master, he researched the cutting of type and the making of paper and ink, indeed every aspect of book production.

The Kelmscott Press was then established in a cottage which Morris rented at 16 Upper Mall, close to Kelmscott House at number 26, on 12 January 1891. When, in a few months, more room was needed, 14 Upper Mall was leased and then in 1894, a third house, 21 Upper Mall, was taken. A retired compositor and master-printer, William Bowden, was employed to run the Press, every aspect of which was supervised by Morris. The Press's paper was copied from a 15th-century Italian model, and was made entirely from linen. Morris imported the blackest ink he could find from Germany. The books were bound in vellum, made from calfskin, or quarter linen. The illustrations were designed by Burne-Jones, the page decorations and the type by Morris. It took Morris a year to design the 'Golden' type; it was based on a Roman type made in 15th-century Venice and was the first to be used by the Press.

It was shortly after the founding of the press that Morris became seriously ill. Fortunately, the designing of type and the cutting of wood

blocks was work which Morris could do while convalescing, even in bed if necessary; the 'Troy' type, based on the Gothic types used by early German printers, was designed in Folkestone, where he and Jenny spent most of the summer of 1891 recuperating. A further delight was that Morris's friendship with Burne-Jones was now abundantly renewed as they worked together on the books for the Press. They had never been estranged, but Burne-Jones had said of the years of Morris's greatest activity as a socialist: 'We are silent about many things, and we used to be silent about nothing'. Now the old full sympathy between them was restored and the pleasant Sunday morning breakfasts at The Grange, Burne-Jones's house in Fulham, were resumed. These remaining years were happy ones for Morris, surrounded by family and friends and busy on work which he loved. One of his greatest joys was the Kelmscott Chaucer on which Morris and Burne-Jones worked together, Burne-Jones designing the 87 illustrations and Morris cutting the wood-blocks. For it Morris designed his third and last type, the 'Chaucer', a smaller version of his Gothic 'Troy' type. Morris would not be satisfied with less than perfection, and was almost afraid that he would not live to see it completed. Mackail records that the Chaucer was 'three years and four months in actual

the wold and the night is a-cold and thames runs chill
hill but kind & dear is the old house here
is warm midst winter's harm rest then & rest: and think

LEFT *One of the hangings on Morris's bed at Kelmscott Manor.*

RIGHT *Photograph of Edward Burne-Jones and William Morris by Hollyer about 1890. The two friends grew closer during the 1890s.*

LEFT *Kelmscott* Chaucer, *page showing a Burne-Jones wood-cut illustration to 'The Clerk's Tale', page ornamentation and 'Chaucer' type by Morris, 1896.*

RIGHT **Hammersmith** *carpet, Morris and Company. In the early days of the Firm's carpet production, Morris often did a great deal of hand-knotting himself; in his insistence that the designer should have technical knowledge of the medium for which he was designing Morris set a personal example which was followed by many Arts and Crafts designers.*

preparation and execution ... the printing ... occupied a year and nine months'; finally on 2 June 1896, only four months before Morris's death in October 1896, the first two copies, one for Morris and one for Burne-Jones, arrived from the binder. 'My eyes! How good it is', said Morris.

The Kelmscott Press never made a profit, and was not intended to. Morris ran it purely for pleasure. As the books were hand-printed, print runs were necessarily short and labour costs high. Only the best materials were used. The Press produced 53 titles, including the chapter entitled 'The Nature of Gothic', from The Stones of Venice by Ruskin, which, since Morris had first read it as an undergraduate in the 1850s, had so much influenced his thinking about art and its relationship to society. The Press was wound up in 1898, two years after Morris's death. Despite its short life, its influence was considerable and it was certainly a precursor of the private press revival, both in Britain and the United States. Although the Kelmscott Press books have sometimes been criticized for unreadability, Morris's work nevertheless inspired publishers, such as JM Dent, who produced the Everyman series, to print commercial work of a higher quality and had generally a beneficent influence on 20th-century typography and book design.

Also published by the Kelmscott Press were some of Morris's own late prose romances, in-cluding The Story of the Glittering Plain, the first book to be published by the Press in May 1891, The Wood Beyond the World (1894) and The Well at the World's End (1896). Like the work of the Press itself, these romances were undertaken simply for Morris's own satisfaction, with no concern to please a contemporary readership; in fact, they were not well received by contemporaries, who criticized his use of obscure and archaic language. There has recently been a revival of critical interest in them and they have probably never been as popular as they are today – especially with a generation brought up on JRR Tolkien. Set in a generalized medieval past, they take the form of fables in which humanity's relationship with the natural world and the balance and tension between the masculine and the feminine are explored in a series of adventures or quests, which are resolved through human courage and endeavour. The women in these stories – with their comradely qualities, their intelligence and their physical energy – reflect Morris's forward-looking views; he told Bernard Shaw that he 'did not consider a man a socialist at all who is not prepared to admit the equality of women'.

Even in his declining years, Morris's creative energy was considerable. Nevertheless, he was aging rapidly, and one Sunday early in 1896 Burne-Jones was alarmed to see that 'in the very middle of breakfast, Morris began leaning his forehead on his hand, as he does so often now. It is a thing I have never seen him do before in all the years I have known him'. A diagnosis of diabetes was confirmed and Mackail notes that by February 'a journey round his garden at Hammersmith was enough to tire him'. His last visit to Kelmscott Manor was made in April and in July, acting on his doctor's advice, he took a sea voyage around the coast of Norway. It was not a success; he was too ill to enjoy it and fretted at being away from his books and manuscripts. On his return he was suffering from congestion of the left lung and it was clear that he was dying.

The last letter written in his own hand was on 1 September to Georgiana Burne-Jones at Rottingdean on the south coast, asking her to, 'Come soon, I want sight of your dear face'. She and Burne-Jones were among the many devoted friends who were constantly with Morris in his last weeks. Mackail relates:

> . . . as the power of self-control slackened, the emotional tenderness which had always been so large an element in his nature became more habitually visible. On one of her latest visits . . . he broke into tears when something was said about the life of the poor. He had a longing to hear for the last time some of that older music for which he had so great an admiration. Mr Arnold Dolmetsch brought down a pair of virginals to Kelmscott House, and played to him several pieces by English composers of the sixteenth century. A pavan and a galliard by William Byrd were what Morris liked most. He broke into a cry of joy at the opening phrase, and after the two pieces had been repeated at his request, was so deeply stirred that he could not bear to hear any more.

Almost his last words were, 'I want to get mumbo-jumbo out of the world'. Between 11 and 12 o'clock on the morning of 3 October, Morris died peacefully; he was 62 years old. A special train was hired to take his body from Paddington to Lechlade. There Cunningham Graham, one of Morris's socialist friends, observed the contrast between Morris's funeral

ABOVE Annesley Lodge, Platts Lane, Hampstead, London, by C F A Voysey, 1895, an example of the small Arts and Crafts house admired by Muthesius. Every detail including the door furniture was designed by the architect.

RIGHT Christening mug for Lord David Cecil made by the Guild of Handicraft in 1902.

and Victorian convention: there were 'no red-faced men in shabby black to stagger with the coffin to the hearse but in their place four countrymen in moleskin bore the body to an open hay cart festooned with vines, with alder and with bullrushes'. The coffin was of un-polished oak with wrought-iron handles. From Lechlade it was taken to Kelmscott, where Morris was buried. The grave is marked by a simple stone designed by Philip Webb. 'My coat feels thinner', said Webb, '. . . one would think I had lost a buttress'. The sense of loss and the great respect and affection which was felt for Morris, particularly by fellow socialists, are summed up by Robert Blatchford, a member of the Independent Labour Party and editor of the socialist paper, the *Clarion*:

> *I cannot help feeling that it does not matter what goes into the* Clarion *this week, because William Morris is dead. And what Socialist will care for any other news this week, beyond that one sad fact? . . . . He was our best man, and he is dead . . . . It is true that much of his work still lives, and will live. But we have lost him, and, great as was his work, he himself was greater . . . . Though his words fell like sword strokes, one always felt that the warrior was stronger than the sword. For Morris was not only a genius, he was a man. Strike him where you would, he rang true . . .*

Morris was not forgotten by working-class socialists. Streets and socialist halls were named after him, and in *The Work of William Morris*, Paul Thompson records how, 'nearly fifty years later, in the great slump, Harold Laski found copies of *The Dream of John Ball* and *News from Nowhere* "in house after house of the miners", even when most of the furniture had been sold'. Perhaps Morris's greatest contri-bution to the socialist movement was the in-spiration which he provided, as Blatchford suggested, more as a man than as a theorist. In fact, the future for British socialism lay not in revolution, as Morris had thought, but in a gentler, reformist approach, specifically through the election to Parliament of the

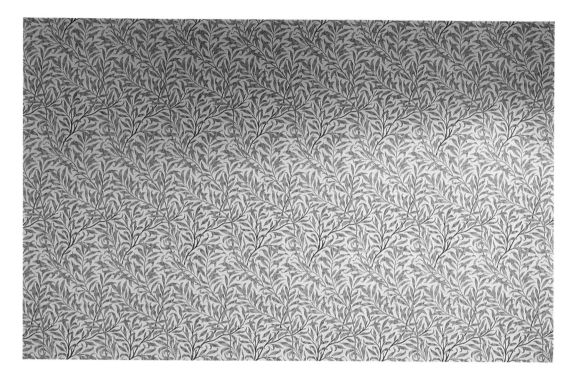

RIGHT *'Willow Boughs' wallpaper, 1887, by Morris.*

Independent Labour Party candidates. Nevertheless, the Socialist League in its short life played a vital part in the forming of the Independent Labour Party; its stronghold was in the north, and from these roots the Party sprang. The Social Democratic Federation was strongest in the south.

Morris did to some extent succeed in educating the working classes in socialism, even though the results were not exactly what he would have hoped. It is more difficult to assess Morris's influence on socialism and socialist thought in the longer term. Recent revaluations of his political writings suggest that Morris's contribution in this area may have been underestimated and that he was a more substantial political theorist than has been realized. EP Thompson suggests that Morris's essential contribution to British socialism was his stress on a moral and humane element, on the importance of community and fellowship, and that this was a necessary complement to the more cerebral Marxist economic analysis.

Morris's reputation in his own lifetime was greatest as a poet: after Tennyson's death in 1892, he was offered, but refused, the Poet Laureateship. Ironically, it is his work as a poet which has worn least well. *The Earthly Paradise*, for which he was most famous in his own day, is now little read and is not highly regarded; by contrast, *The Defence of Guenevere and Other Poems*, which was poorly received by Morris's contemporaries, is now seen as surprisingly innovative, in some ways anticipating the Symbolist poetry of later in the century.

The firm of Morris and Company continued under the management of Dearle, but its best work was done in Morris's lifetime. It can be argued that Morris's greatest influence was as a designer, in particular in the contribution which he made to the Arts and Crafts Movement – a term which, embracing an enormous variety and disparity of style and technique, refers essentially to a spirit and an ethos. Morris insisted that work which is produced by hand, allowing the craftsman or woman his

LEFT 'Strawberry Thief' printed cotton, indigo discharged, designed by Morris, registered at the Patent Office May 1883.

RIGHT 'Bachelor's Button' wallpaper, designed by Morris, 1892, one of his few late wallpapers.

or her creative contribution, is morally and aesthetically superior to the machine-made: it was this philosophy which lay at the heart of the Arts and Crafts Movement. Morris's role in raising the status of the applied arts was vital, as was his insistence that the designer should have technical knowledge of the medium for which he or she was designing. In this respect he set a personal example which was followed by many Arts and Crafts designers.

The idea of the guild, with its medieval precedents and connotions of dignity and independence, was taken up by CR Ashbee (1863–1942), an architect, designer and writer, who established the Guild and School of Handicraft in London in 1888. Like Morris, Ashbee preferred to take unskilled men and train them himself in emulation of the medieval system of apprenticeship to a guild, but he went beyond Morris in introducing a profit-sharing scheme for his workers in 1898. Just as Morris had moved his factory out to Merton Abbey in 1881, so Ashbee moved the Guild's workshops out to the Cotswolds in 1902, enabling his workmen to live and work in a rural community. Another influential disciple of Morris was the architect WR Lethaby (1857–1931), who took up Morris's emphasis on the

importance of education in the crafts; with the sculptor, George Frampton, he set up the London Central School of Arts and Crafts in the 1890s and was its first director. It was the first school to acknowledge the importance of the crafts by establishing workshops for them, and so assisting the spread of Arts and Crafts principles.

It was no coincidence that the main figures of the Arts and Crafts Movement were usually architects, for Morris regarded the applied arts as the natural and essential complement to architecture. The Movement was particularly influential in domestic architecture; in this sphere the work of CFA Voysey (1857–1941) was especially distinguished. After Morris, Voysey was perhaps the most impressive and innovative designer of the Arts and Crafts Movement. Like Morris a prodigious worker and a prolific designer, he was concerned with every form of applied art, designing everything for his houses from textiles to door-knockers. His work followed Morris's in being informed by a knowledge of technique; one often sees technical instructions to the manufacturer written by Voysey on his designs. Occasionally there is an echo of a Morris design in his work; 'Bird and Berries' surely owes something to 'The Strawberry Thief', even though the more muted colours and greater stylization stamp it with Voysey's very distinctive quality. Voysey adopted and developed Morris's insistence on simplicity, unpretentiousness and an honest use of materials; this is seen, for instance, in Morris's innovative use of a plain kitchen table of scrubbed wood at Kelmscott House and in the white-washed walls at Kelmscott Manor. Voysey popularized this rustic and puritanical style through the publication of his designs in the Arts and Crafts periodical, The Studio. These designs became extremely influential on the Continent through their publication in Das Englishe Haus (1904–05) by Hermann Muthesius (1861–1927), a great

LEFT 'Bird and Berries', printed cotton, designed by C F A Voysey.

S·CECILIA

RIGHT St. Cecilia, stained glass panel designed by Burne-Jones, about 1872–73, made by Morris and Company about 1897. Many of the Company's early designs continued to be used by the Firm well into the twentieth century.

admirer of the work of Voysey, Ashbee and other English domestic architects. In the United States publications such as *International Studio* and *The Craftsman* caused Arts and Crafts ideas and designs to be widely known.

In 1907 Muthesius founded the *Deutscher Werkbund*, a group of progressive German and Austrian designers, whose intent was to revitalize German design by bringing together architects, craftsmen and manufacturers. To Morris's understanding of the social importance of design and concern for honest use of materials was added a new awareness of the potential of industrial production. Although most of the products of the *Deutscher Werkbund* appear similar to those of the Arts and Crafts Movement, there was the beginning of an ideological rift as the emphasis shifted from hand-craftsmanship to mass-production by machine. This underlying philosophical difference became further evident in subsequent developments such as the Bauhaus and what has come to be known as the Modern Movement in architecture and design. Although Morris is often regarded as one of the precursors of Modernism, it is likely he would have found its obsession with functionalism and with forms inspired by machine-production antipathetic; certainly Le Corbusier's vision of mass accommodation in tower-blocks was contrary to everything Morris believed in. The concept of the garden city, anticipated by Morris's lectures on architecture, was a far more genuine development of his concern that art and architecture should never ignore human individuality and the vital relationship with the natural world.

Morris's influence persists to the present day in many spheres. The Society for the Protection of Ancient Buildings, founded largely by Morris in 1878, is still active today and was the forerunner of many other societies devoted to conservation. His work as a designer is almost as popular as it was at the height of the

LEFT *'Tulip and Rose' woven cloth, designed by Morris, registered in 1876. Morris's use of naturalistic forms in textile design was taken up by the Arts and Crafts movement.*

Arts and Crafts Movement. The tradition of the designer-craftsman is still a strong and vital one. Perhaps Morris was most prescient in his awareness that people cannot flourish unless they protect and are in harmony with their environment. He was a visionary who dreamt of art flourishing in a free and equal society; in his 1877 lecture, 'The Lesser Arts of Life', Morris declared:

*I do not want art for a few, any more than education for a few, or freedom for a few . . . art will make our streets as beautiful as the wood, as elevating as mountain-sides: it will be a pleasure and a rest . . . to come from the open country into a town; every man's house will be fair and decent, soothing to his mind and helpful to his work: all the works of man that we live amongst and handle will be in harmony with nature, will be reasonable and beautiful . . . in no private dwelling will there be any signs of waste, pomp, or insolence, and every man will have his share of the* best.

# INDEX

## FURTHER INFORMATION ABOUT
## WILLIAM MORRIS

The best William Morris collections are held by the Victoria and Albert Museum, London, and the William Morris Gallery, Walthamstow, which was also Morris's boyhood home. The Red House, Red House Lane, Bexley Heath, Kent, and Kelmscott Manor, near Lechlade, Gloucestershire may be visited by appointment. The William Morris Society has its headquarters in the basement of Kelmscott House, 26 Upper Mall, Hammersmith, London W6 9TA. The Society is always happy to answer queries about Morris. It has a programme of events and publishes a quarterly *Newsletter* and a *Journal*. It has members all over the world and publishes a North American newsletter.

## SELECTED FURTHER READING ABOUT
## MORRIS AND HIS CIRCLE

GEORGIANA BURNE-JONES, *Memorials of Edward Burne-Jones* 2 vols. (London, 1904)

GH CROW, *William Morris, Designer* (London, 1934)

PETER FAULKNER, *Against the Age: An Introduction to William Morris* (London, 1980)

PENELOPE FITZGERALD, *Edward Burne-Jones, A Biography* (London, 1975)

PHILIP HENDERSON, *William Morris, His Life, Work and Friends* (London, 1967)

WR LETHABY, *Philip Webb and his Work* (London, 1935)

JW MACKAIL, *The Life of William Morris* 2 vols. (London, 1899)

JAN MARSH, *Jane and May Morris: A Biographical Story 1839–1938* (London, 1986)

MAY MORRIS, *William Morris: Artist, Writer, and Socialist* (Oxford, 1936)

*William Morris: Selected Writings*, edited by GDH Cole (London, 1948)

WILLIAM MORRIS: *Selected Writings and Designs*, edited by Asa Briggs (London, 1962, frequent reprints)

*The Collected Letters of William Morris*, edited by Norman Kelvin, 3 vols. (Princeton, New Jersey, 1984)

GILLIAN NAYLOR, *William Morris by Himself* (London, 1988)

LINDA PARRY, *William Morris Textiles* (London, 1983)

EP THOMPSON, *William Morris: Romantic to Revolutionary* (London, 1955)

PAUL THOMPSON, *The Work of William Morris* (London, 1977)

AC SEWTER, *The Stained Glass of William Morris and his Circle* 2 vols. (London, 1974–5)

RAY WATKINSON, *William Morris as a Designer* (1967)

## PICTURE CREDITS